A Lifes JOURNEY

An Inspirational
Poetry Collection

CONNIE COLEMAN

AuthorHouse™
1663 Liberty Drive
Bloomington, IN 47403
www.authorhouse.com
Phone: 1 (800) 839-8640

Published by AuthorHouse 08/18/2015

ISBN: 978-1-5049-3243-1 (sc)
ISBN: 978-1-5049-3242-4 (e)

Print information available on the last page.

Contents

PROSE; LONG POEMS; STORY POEMS

"A Glimpse of Jordon"

THE LIGHT SHONE SO BRIGHT AND CLEAR
AS I GLIMPSED JORDAN'S BANKS SO NEAR.
RUSHING THROUGH A BREAK IN ROCKS THERE
WATER POURED OUT, DOWN; BLESSING EARTHS' SPHERE.

HOW THIS COULD BE I DID NOT KNOW
EXCEPT THAT OUR LORD DEEMED IT SO!
I WISHED THERE TO STAY, NEVER GO……
I CRAVED TO SEE MY JESUS' FACE SO:

TO HEAR THE MASTERS VOICE SO DEAR;
SEE HIS SANDALED FEET THAT WALKED HERE;
TO FOLLOW CLOSE, EVER SO NEAR;
TO FALL AT HIS FEET, MY SAVIOR!

YET I KNEW, THAT WOULD LATER BE.
WONDER EENOUGH, JORDAN TO SEE;
HER RUSHING WATERS COOL AND SWEET
ANS THE GLORIOUS SWEET PEACE!

"All the Simple Wonders"

I THINK OF ALL THE SIMPLE,
BEAUTIFUL WONDERS GOD HAS GIVEN ME.
YET NONE ARE REALLY SIMPLE*1*
WHEN I TAKE A REAL GOOD LOOK JUST TO SEE.

ONLY GOD COULD PLAN EACH
BEAUTIFUL FLOWER PETAL THAT I SEE
AND OH IT WASN'T SIMPLE
WHEN HE PLANNED A HUMAN LIKE YOU AND ME!

FROM A SIMPLE OLD WORM
TO A BUTTERFLY? HUMOR THERE I SEE!
BUT A HUMAN COULD NOT
HAVE MADE SUCH A MAGICAL THING FOR ME!

EACH SIMPLE THING I SEE
IS NOT REALLY SIMPLE YOU SEE.
ONLY THE GREAT CREATOR
COULD HAVE IMAGINED THEM; AND MADE THEM BE!

"Alone"

MANY HAVE FELT LONELY, I HAVE FELT ENTIRELY ALONE
WITH NO HUMAN TO TURN TO, SOLELY ALONE.
ENGULFED IN DEPRESSION, BLACKNESS AROUND ME
I HEARD PEOPLES VOICES, BUT NO ONE DID I SEE.

IN THE MIDST OF OTHERS NO ONE REALLY KNEW ME,
THE SADDNESS INSIDE OR THE TROUBLES THAT I SEE.
TO CARRY THAT LOAD ALL ALONE WEIGHS ONE DOWN.
IT HAD NEARLY DRUG ME TO THE GROUND.

THEN I REMEMBERED A PROMISE THE LORD HAD MADE
I SAW A GLIMMER OF LIGHT, THE DARKNESS INVADE.
THE LORD HAD SAID; "I SHALL NEVER FORSAKE THEE."
BY THAT PROMISE; THE DARKNESS LIFTED, I COULD SEE!

"America, Sweet America"

AMERICA, SWEET AMERICA, YOU ARE OUR OWN LAND.

IN FIGHT FOR YOU HAS DIED MANY A STRONG, GOOD MAN.

OUR FOREFATHERS HELD THE FLAG; PROUDLY PASSED IT ON.

WE WERE PROUD OF OUR LAND; PROUD WHEN BATTLE WAS WON!

OUR AMERICA" LET NOT HER BEAUTY LIE AND RUST

LET US CLEAN THE FLAG, REUNITE; ONCE AGAIN TRUST!

WE'VE LONG BEEN PROUD OF WHAT AMERICA STANDS FOR.

WE HAVE FREEDOM; OPORTUNITY, WEALTH: MUCH MORE!

WE ARE A NATION UNDER GOD: IN HIM RELY!

STOP POLLUTING OUR STATES, GIVE IMPROVEMENT A TRY!

OUR MORALS HAVE LARGELY LESSONED, WITH THEM, OUR PRIDE!

WE NOW NEED TO STAND FOR AMERICASTAND SIDE BY SIDE!

BRING OUT OUR FLAG AND SHAKE LOOSE POLITICAL DUST;

WE NEED TO UNITE AGAIN: WITH, "IN GOD WE TRUST!"

"Angel Sister"

HUMANS PICTURE ONLY WITH MORTAL MIND

SWEET HEEAVENLY THINGS WE THINK MAY "BE;"

KNOWING, THE REAL IMAGE WE CANNOT "SEE."

TO US, HEAVEN, IS BEHIND CLOSED BLINDS!

I DARE NOT SAY WHAT REAL ANGELS ARE LIKE,

THO' IN MIND'S EYE I HAVE PICTURED ONE.

HER BEAUTY I DO LOVE TO DWELL UPON,

AND HAVE TREASURED SINCE A LITTLE TYKE!

YES, SHE WAS PICTURED THIRTY YEARS AGO:

I'M THIRTY SEVEN, SHE'S TWENTY-NINE!

THE ANGEL FROM LONG AGO IN MY MIND:

IS M Y LITTLE SISTER I LOVE SO!

"A Prayer for Church"

OUR FATHER, HERE WE STAND WHERE OTHER

HAVE STOOD, BUT NOW ARE GONE:

PERHAPS HERE STAND A FEW THAT WILL NOT BE

HERE VERY LONG; WE NEVER KNOW!

WITH US ARE SOME NEW FOLLOWERS, WHO HAVE JOINED US BY THE WAY.

MAY GOD BLESS EACH ONE STANDING HERE IN HIS

HOUSE TODAY! TOGETHER MAY WE GROW!

FOR THOSE WHO COULDN'T MAKE IT, BUT

ARE HERE WITHIN THEIR HEARTS,

MAY THEY RECEIVE A BLESSING, THEY'RE

ALSO AN IMPORTNT PART OF THE

"DURBIN FAMILY."

SOMEDAY, MAY, WE ALL STAND TOGETHER UPON

A HIGHER, STURDIER; GROUND:

AND IN HEAVEN, MAY WE EACH AND EVERY ONE BE FOUND AS A BRANCH

ON THE LORDS' FAMILY TREE!

"A Sweet Vision"

(IN ANSWER TO MY NEEDS DURING A YEAR OF MANY
CRISES' HE BLOCKED MOST OF MY PAIN!)

IN THE SPRING OF THAT YEAR MY COUSIN AND MENTOR PASSED

DAD HAD CANCER;

ONLY HAD UNTIL AUGUST TO LAST.

WE ALL DREADED THE PAIN HE WOULD HAVE TO GO THROUGH!

JULY FIRST MY HUSBAND ASKED FOR A DIVORCE TOO!

I HURT SO, MY REAL HEART FELT PAIN! THEN: I SAW SO PLAIN

A FIGURE IN A WHITE ROBE: WITH SOMETHING IS HIS HANDS!

THE ROOM WAS FILLED WITH POWER AND WITH A GREAT PEACE!

OF THE LARGE FIGURE I SAW ONLY NECK TO WAIST.

WHERE HIS HANDS CRADLED 'ROUND, BUT DID NOT TOUCH, AN ORB

WHICH SPUN AND FOATED WITHIN THE HANDS OF THE LORD!

LOVE ISSUED FROM HIM TO OUR PRECIOUS SPINNING WORLD!

HE CRADLED GENTLY HIS OWN CREATION, "A-WHIRL"!

HE HOLDS SAFE ALL THE EARTH! ALL LIFE LIES WITHIN HIS HANDS!

AS HE LOVES THE PRECIOUS WORLD; ALSO HE LOVES MAN!

LET HIM TAKE AWAY YOUR DESOLATION, YOUR PAIN

HE IS THERE TO RESCUE US; AGAIN AND AGAIN!

"Attitudes"

AT TIMES WITH PROUD ATTITUDES, WE WALK WITHOUT GOD.

AT TIME WITHOUT SERVITUDE, SELFISHLY WE TROD.

OUR BROTHERS IN SOLITUDE, CRY: "HELP ME;" IN VAIN.

THE BROKEN AND BRUISED, IN ANGUISH; ONLY KNOW PAIN.

JESUS AT GETHSEMANE, GROANED IN PRAYER; ALONE.

HE WAS TO SACRIFICE HIS LIFE FOR OUR SINS SOON!

HE HAD NO PROUD ATTITUDE; HE SERVED, DIED FOR MAN!

HE CHOSE TO SHED HIS BLOOD TO PAY FOR ALL OUR SINS.

THE BROKEN AND BRUISED HE CARED FOR; OFT' WITHOUT SLEEP!

BEFORE RISING TO HEAVEN HE SAID; "FEED MY SHEEP!"

DYING; "FATHER FORGIVE THEM;" UNSELFISHLY; HE PRAYED!

HE GAVE HIS LIFE, SHED HIS BLOOD THAT WE MAY BE SAVED!

"DARE WE"

DARE WE? AFTER GOD HAS SENT HIS ONLY SON DOWN:

HIS SON SACRIFICED HIMSELF FOR US LIKE A LAMB:

CARRY PROUD ATTITUDES AND WALK WITHOT OUR GOD;

NOT FEED HIS SHEEP; AND HERE ON EARTH SELFISHLY TROD?

"Aunt Letttie"

I USED TO READ HER A LOVE POEM NOW AND THEN,

SHE APPRECIATED SWEET WORDS FROM A PEN.

TO MANY, HER GRACIOUSNESS OVER FLOWED:

I WANT TO DEDICATE TO HER THIS LITTLE ODE!

BE STRANGER, LOVED ONE OR FRIEND IN NEED,

SHE BEFRIENDED EACH WITH A SPECIAL WORD OR DEED!

TO HER HOME AND HER HEART SHE TOOK IN MANY.

SHE ALWAYS PREPARED FROM HER CUPBOARD FOOD FOR PLENTY'

WHEN I WAS A CHILD SHE SEEMED A LITTLE STERN TO ME,

BUT 'TWAS ONLY STANDING UP FOR RIGHT YOU SEE.

HER LOVE WAS EVENLY GIVEN TO YOUNG AND OLD.

SHE SHARED HER LIFE WITH ALL THE FOLD.

NOW SHE RESTS WITH HER LOVED ONES BY JESUS' SIDE.

HER LIFE HERE ON EARTH CAN BE REMEMBERED WITH PRIDE!

THIS WOMAN WHO STOOD SO TALL AND STRAIGHT AND PROUD;

I'VE LOVED HER DEARLY SINCE I WAS A CHILD!

I'M PROUD TODAY THAT SHE WAS MY GREAT AUNT

AS I ALWAYS FELT SHE WAS MOST LIKE A SAINT!

"Aunt Nellie"

I WRITE VERSE, SOME SAY I TOY WITH MY TIME.

'OFT I HAVE STRANGE DREAMS.

BUT THERE IS GOOD TO BE SAID OF RHYME.

'OFT TRUTH IN A DREAM IS SEEN!

I REMEMBER DREAMEING AROUND (1976), OF A

FAMILY REUNION AT JACOBSON PARK.

MY FAMILY WAS ALL THERE, WE WERE SIX: WITH

A GOOD MANY OTHERS AT THE PARK.

WE CHATTERED, CHILDREN PLAYED. ALL WAS

CALM, THE SUN WAS SHINNING BRIGHT.

I TURNED TO THROW A PAPER PLATE AWAY AS I

HEARD A HORN BLOW, OUT OF SIGHT.

THE SOUND GREW NEARER AND LOUDER.

PEOPLE TURNED TO FIND THE SOUND.

THEN SUDDDENLY THERE WAS QUITE A TO-DO;

PEOPLE LOOKING UP AND MULLING ROUND.

I WONDERED; "IS IT GABRIEL:" LOOKED UP AND

SAW CLOUDS MOVING WAY UP HIGH!

WHITE CLOUDS BILLOWED AND SURE ENOUGH, MIDST

THE FAR AWAY CLOUDS; JESUS LIT UP THE SKY!

I CALLED TO THE CHILDREN TO COME ALONG. I SAW

AUNT NELLIE THERE SLOSE TO MY SIDE'

HER FAMILY WAS COMING TOO. WE HEARD MUSIC AND SONG.

LOOKING UP WE SAW THE ANGELS AROUND JESUS', ON ALL SIDES!

AUNT NELLIE SMILED THAT LITTLE PROUD SMILE

FOR WHICH SHE IS WELL KNOWN.

THEN, BRINGING FROM HER POCKET THE WHILE,

A TINY CHANGE BAG SHE OWNED.

STANDING PROPER, BACK HELD STRAIGHT;

EYES GLEAMING, SO VERY PLEASED

TO BE PREPARED AHEAD, NOT TO BE LATE: AUNT

NELLIE SIMPLY SAID TO ME, "I HAVE MY KEY!"

I WOKE UP, YET I KNEW IF MORE SHE SPOKE IT

WOULD BE LIKE: "DRY THIOSE TEARS."

"MAKE SURE YOUR KEY IS IN YOUR COAT, I'LL

SEE YOU SOON NOW, YOU HEAR?"

OF COURSE SHE WOULD BE PASSING ON UP AHEAD

TO THE STEPS TO PRESENT HER KEY.

IN THAT DREAM THERE WERE STEPS GOING UP INTO

THE SKY PAST THE CLOUDS FOR YOU AND FOR ME!

"Aunt Sis-Sis"

SOMEONE SPECIAL CAME FROM WAY OUT WEST,

AND MADE MY LITTLE CHILDREN HER PETS!

SHE WOULD CROCHET BLANKETS WITH THEIR NAME.

SHE WOULD PUT THEIR NAMES IN SONGS, SHE SANG.

TO US ALL SHE MEANT SO VERY MUCH

SHE GAVE LIFE THAT EXTRA SPECIAL TOUCH!

SHE LAUGHED AND WAS LOTS OF FUN!

THE CHILDREN WOULD PICK ON HER, THEN RUN!

SHE WAS JUST "SPECIAL," THAT LADY FINE.

I'M GLAD THEY KNEW THAT SWEET AUNT OF MINE.

WE ARE GLAD SHE CAME FROM WAY OUT WEST!

THAT SPECIAL, SPECIAL, AUNT SIS-SIS!

"Baby Don't You Cry"

WHAT HAPPENED TO THE BABE

THST SWEET INNOCENT BABE

I ROCKED TO SLEEP AT NIGHT

THOUGHT I TAUGHT TO DO RIGHT!

LORI LEIGH, LORI LEIGH, HE JUST LIED. HUSH NOW BABY,

DON'T YOU CRY!

BYE OH BABY, BYE OH BYE, HUSH NOW BABY,

HUSH NOW BABY, DON'T YOU CRY!

YOU GOTTA' WATCH A BOY

HE'LL USE YOU FOR A TOY

NEVER STOP TO THINK

JUST WINE, WOMEN, DRINK!

LORI LEIGH, LORI LEIGH, HE JUST LIED. HUSH NOW BABY,

DON'T YOU CRY!

BYE OH BABY, BYE OH BYE, HUSH NOW BABY,

HUSH NO BABY, DON'T YOU CRY!

PRETTY YOUNG THING

HE GAVE YOU A RING

YOU THOUGHT THAT WAS NICE

DIDN'T KNOW THE PRICE!

LORI LEIGH, LORI LEIGH, HE JUST LIED. HUSH NOW BABY,

DON'T YOU CRY!

BYE OH BABY, BYE OH BYE, HUSH NOW BABY,

HUSH NOW BABY, DON'T YOU CRY!

HE'S HARDENED YOUR HEART

BROKEN IT APART,

BURST YOUR BUBBLE IN THE SKY

HUSH BABY, DON'T CRY!

LORI LEIGH, LORI LEIGH, HE JUST LIED. HUSH NOW BABY,

DON'T YOU CRY!

BYE OH BABY. BYE OH BYE, HUSH NOW BABY,

HUSH NOW BABY, DON'T YOU CRY!

"Bee a Bee"

BE A SHINING SUNBEAM

BE A BUSY LITTLE BEE.

SHOW THE LOVE OF JESUS

BUZZING WHOEVER YOU SEE.

BE A BIRD OF MESSAGE

PASS THE STORY "JESUS CAME;"

HOW HE LOVED GODS' CHILDREN

AND DIED FOR OUR SINS IN PAIN.

BE A CHANGED BUTTERFLY

FLITTING ABOUT WITH LOVE:

WHO WAS ONCE A WIGGLY WORM

BEFORE GROWING WINGS WE LOVE!

TOTE THE GOSPEL STORY.

CARRY IT WITH A BIG SMILE;

HOW HE LIVED, DIED, AROSE

TO PAY FOR OUR SINS SO VILE.

BE A SHINNING LITTLE SUNBEAM

BE A BUSY BEE….

HE'S BUILDING IN HEAVEN.

A HOME FOR YOU AND ME!

"Beautiful Lady of My Childhood Dreams"

YOUR WORDS BRING BACK MANY MEMORIES

OF DREAMS I'VE FORGOTTEN SINCE CHILDHOOD DAYS.

YOUR HEART IS FULL OF INNOCENCE AND GOODNESS

YOUR WAYS INNOCENT AS MY LOST CHILDHOOD WAYS!

IN NATURE, YOU SEE MORE THAN OTHERS SEE;

AND YOUR HEART; DREAMS, AS MINE ONCE DREAMED.

YOU KEEP ON DREAMING, MY DREAMS HAVE STRAYED.

YOU ARE TO ME AS I SHOULD HAVE STAYED!

YOU LOVE THE VERY SIMPLE THINGS IN LIFE.

YOU CAN BE HAPPY WITHOUT MUCH AT ALL.

THE SIMPLE THINGS HAVE LESSENED TO ME

AND HAPPINESS TO ME TODAY DOTH CALL.

TO DREAM LIKE YOU, MY LIFE AWAY

WOULD MAKE ME HAPPY EACH DAY.

EDDIE, EDDIE, SO VERY SWEET AND KIND,

HOW SUCH A FRIEND DID I EVER FIND?

"Beauty"

"WHAT IS THIS FEELING?" "I CANNOT EXPLAIN."

"IT COST NOT A SHILLING; IT'S A GREAT GAIN."

"BEAUTY I CAN SEE EVERYWHERE I LOOK!"

"SUCH BEAUTY AND PEACE OF MIND I HAVE FOUND!"

"BEAUTY; OH YES, MINE: ONCE I LOOK AROUND"

"OH SILLY, SILLY ME." "IT'S BEEN HERE ALL THE TIME!"

"GOD PLACED IT HERE FOR ALL OF US TO FIND!"

"Beauty is My Duty"

I JUST SIT HERE FOR HOURS ENJOYING THE BEAUTY.

I CONSIDER DOING SO IS MY OWN PERSONAL DUTY.

THIS PLACE BECAME MINE FROM AN ACT OF GOD,

SO TAKING IN EACH DETAIL IS MY LITTLE JOB.

HOW JOYOUS TO SEE A BLUEBIRD OUT THE WINDOW PANE

AND PUT FOOD OUT FOR THE FINCHES WHEN IT RAINS!

THE CARDINAL IS A SPECIAL COLORFUL DELIGHT;

THE LITTLE SWALLOWS LOOK SO MINI IN FLIGHT!

THIS HOUSE BUILT JUST SO, DOWN RIVER HILL;

LETS ME SEE THE TOPS OF THE TREES FROM MY WINDOW SILL.

NOW IT'S SNOWING AND FOR THE FIRST TIME I SEE

HOW THE SNOW DRIFTS DOWN TO COVER A TREE!

THE GROUND WON'T BE COVERED FOR SOME TIME

BUT I'LL STILL BE SITTING AT THIS PERCH OF MINE!

WAITING AWAY MY DAY SOME WOULD SAY…..

BUT ONLY DOING MY DUTY…BEAUTY AS MY PAY.

"Beauty of a Girl"

OH THE BEAUTY OF THE CHILD, A GIRL. THE
MUSIC IN HER INNOCENT PLAY
THE SONG, THE LILT, THE PLAYFUL SWIRL THE
PROUD STANCE, THE BASHFUL SWAY.
A BUTTERCUP IN THE SPRINGS MORNING DEW HER
JOY AND LUGHTER SWEET AND CLEAR.
HER BEING: SO FRESH, SO INNOCENT, SO NEW,
HER PRESENCE MAKING LIFE SO DEAR.
A ROSE BUD, TINY, A PRECIOUS BABY THING,
GROWTH AND BEAUTY YET TO UNFOLD.
BUT BEFORE FULL GROWTH AND BEAUTY, A
TINY ROSEBUD SWEET TO HOLD.
A PEARL DROP FRESH FROM THE SALTY SEA,
SHINY AND BEAUTIFUL TO THE EYE
PURE, PERFECT, INNOCENT, A WONDER TO SEE.
SWEET YET TART, NO ONE KNOWS WHY!
MORE PRECIOUS THAN DIAMONDS BABY GIRL,
MOLDED AND SHAPED BY GODS' HAND.
NOTHING MORE LOVED IN THE WHOLE WIDE WORLD;
A BABE TO GROW TO WOMAN FOR MAN!
OH WHAT COULD BE MORE CHERISHED IN ALL THE
WORLD, MORE PRECIOUS THAN DIAMONDS EVEN,
THAN LIVELY, LOVELY, INNOCENT, NEW, UNFURLED;
GEM OF A FLOWER, A GIRL SENT FROM HEAVEN!
AND I HAVE BEEN SENT FOUR!

"Be Kind and Gentle"

BE KIND AND GENTLE WHATEVER YOU DO,

WHEREVER YOU MAY BE.

SOMETHING I WAS ASKED TO DO,

IT'S SO IMPORTANT TO ME.

THESE WORDS WERE SOFTLY SPOKEN

YET CARRY SO MUCH WEIGHT I SAW.

NOW THEY ARE MY TOKEN,

THEY MEAN SO MUCH TO ALL.

THEY ARE MUCH LIKE JESUS' WORDS,

PLEASE REMEMBER HIS CALL.

THE WORLD WOULD BE A BETTER PLACE

IF REMEMBERED BY ALL.

THE KIND AND GENTLE,

THEY ARE LOVED THE BEST.

LET IT BE YOUR TOKEN

YOU WILL BE BLESSED.

"Bible"

THE BIBLE HAS A CERTAIN WAY

TO GIVE NEW MEANING TO EACH DAY.

AND IF ONLY ONE WOULD LOOK;

IT IS THE MOST INTERESTING BOOK.

GREATER KNOWLEDE NOWHERE ELSE IS FOUND.

GREATER LOVE, IN NO OTHER PAGES BOUND!

GREATER TRUTH NOWHERE ELSE IS TOLD,

THAN IN ITS' PAGES BOUND IN GOLD!

"Birth and Death"

EACH TIME THERE IS A BIRTH

THERE MUST COME A HURT!

EACH TIME THERE IS A DEATH

THERE WILL COME TRUE REST!

"Birth of a Christian"

WHO CAN PUT IN WORDS THE BEAUTY OF BIRTH?

A FLOWER COMES FORTH FROM PLAIN LOOKING EARTH

THEN SOFT COLORED PETALS COME, VELVET AND PURE.

WORDS CAN'T RELAY THE ESSENCE OF THEIR ALLURE.

A COLT IS BORN ON A COLD WINTER DAY

THE MARE NUZZLES IT AND IT SOFTLY NEIGHS.

WHO CAN EXPLAIN THEIR BEAUTY SIDE BY SIDE

OR FEEL THE MARES' LOVE AND SWEEET SILENT PRIDE?

A PEACH BLOSSOM TASTES BITTER TO THE TONGUE

AS DOTH THE RIPE FRUIT WHEN IT IS TOO YOUNG

YET SOMEHOW THE BITTER FRUIT WILL GROW SWEET

AND BE A FRUIT DELICIOUS TO EAT.

BUT TONGUE CANNOT TELL HOW A SWEET MAIDEN

FROM CHILD TO BRIDE, TO A MOTHER IS LADEN.

A MAGIC BEAUTY FALLS UPON A TEEN.

A MOTHER HOLDING A NEW BABE IS QUEEN!

BUT HOW JESUS ENTERS INTO A HEART

AND AT ONCE FROM SIN THAT HEART TURNS APART

THEN FILLS WITH JESUS' STORY TO IMPART:

IS A RIDDLE KNOWN ONLY IN THAT ONE'S HEART!

"Bonnie"

I ONCE WISHED JUST TO BE
A HAPPY LITTLE BUBBLE OUT IN THE BLUE SEA
ROLLING AND SPLASHING ALONG ALL DAY
A DEEP LAUGHTER BUBBLE, IN THE OCEAN SPRAY!

MY FIRST BORN DAUGHTER YOU ARE.
I SEE IN YOU MUCH I'VE REACHED OUT FOR,
BECOME REAL IN YOU MY DARLING, MY OWN;
BEING SO MUCH LIKE THE WISHES I'VE KNOWN.

YOUR DEEP HAPPY LAUGHTER, SO FREE
SEEMS THE LAUGHTER HELD BACK FOR YEARS IN ME.
THE THINGS YOU SAY AND THE THINGS YOU DO
SEEM THINGS I WISHED I COULD DO TOO.

SOMEHOW A PART OF ME HIDDEN
I COULD NOT SEEM TO SHOW; WAS SWEETLY GIVEN
BY GOD TO YOU, JUST FOR ME TO SEE AND KNOW
TO LOVE AND ENJOY, EVEN TO WATCH GROW.

YOU ARE THE FREE, HAPPY PART OF ME;
THAT LITTLE BUBBLE, ROLLING IN THE BLUE SEA
SWEET PURE LAUGHTER THAT FLOWS
CARRYING WARMTH AND JOY TO OTHERS SOULS!

FROM MAMA

"Bonnie, Misty, Stephanie, Glenda"

BONNIE IS MY CUTE LITTLE DAISY,

HAPPY, BUBBLING AND FULL OF FUN.

SUNSHINE BRIGHT IS HER NATURE;

SMILING LIKE THE MORNING SUN.

MISTY IS MY RARE, RARE ORCHID;

SWEET, MYSTICAL EXOTIC FLOWER,

CERTAINLY THE ONLY ONE OF HER KIND;

FULL OF LIVING AND FULL OF FIRE.

STEPHANIE IS MY TOUCH ME NOT;

YET, CREATING TOGETHERNESS ALL THE TIME.

SHE GROWS IN BEAUTY PERFECTLY IF LEFT ALONE:

A CHILD AFTER THIS HEART OF MINE.

GLENDA IS JUST SO VERY SWEET

A KINDER HEART YOU WILL NEVER FIND.

FLOWING WITH TALENTS, RARE TO MEET;

BUT JUST MY LITTLE CHILD AT SOME TIMES!

"Brianna"

THE LORD CREATED THE EARTH, MOON AND STARS, LAND AND SEA.

I PRAY THE FATHER OF ALL WILL LOOK DOWN ON THEE.

I PRAY HE HAS COMPASSION UPON YOUR YOUNG LIFE,

SENDS YOU HELP AND MERCY FOR YOUR

STRIFE!

MAY THE ANGELS EVER PLEAD HELP AND MERCY FOR THEE

AND MAY A MIRACLE COME FROM THE FATHER ABOVE WHO SEES.

HE WHO MADE THE LILY, HE WHO MADE THE ROSE,

HE CAN SEND A MIRACLE, AND OUR FATHER KNOWS!

MAY HIS WILL BE DONE AND VICTORY WON. I PRAY IT BE HIS WILL

AMEN!

"Bubble"

GREATER THAN POESY CAN 'ERE EXPRESS:

OH THE HEAVENLY, WONDEROUS HAPPINESS

OF FREEDOM!

OH BUT COULD I JUST BE

AS FREE AS THE BUBBLE UPON THE SEA:

FLOATING SO SOFTLY, THEN, SLIDING O'ER THE WAVE!

GAINING SPEED....

LEAPING INTO THE CAVE

OF DARKNESS

'NEATH THE SEA:

THEN....OUT AGAIN; IN, OUT AGAIN, I'D BE

FASTER THAN THE TWINKLING EVEN OF AN EYE!

OH SWEET LIFE!!!

WOULD IT...

WERE I

"Carol"

THERE IS SOMETHING MAGIC HIDDEN IN YOU:

WHY, IT'S THAT PRETTY SMILE YOU WEAR;

AND IF ONCE A YEAR I FIND YOU BLUE

IT SOMEHOW MANAGES TO RETURN THERE!

YOU SEEM TO ME, A BRIGHT, SHINING STAR;

ALWAYS MAKING LIFE A LITTLE BRIGHTER.

IT MATTERS NOT DEAR CAROL, WHERE YOU ARE

THAT STAR GROWS BRIGHTER AND BRIGHTER!

"Cherish the Child"

THE OLDER ONE BECOMES,

FASTER AND SWEETER CHILDREN GROW.

SO MOTHERS WHILE THEY ARE HOME

CHERISH YOUR TIME, WALK VERY SLOW.

CHERISH THE SWEET PINK CHEEK

THE SWEET BABY SMILE THAT SO QUICKLY GOES,

THE HAND THAT WITH YOURS LINKS,

AND THE ROUND PUDGY LITTLE TOES.

COLLECT SQUEEZES AND HUGS.

TEACH THEM ALL THEY NEED TO KNOW.

TUCK THEM IN VERY SNUG

AT NIGHT AND KISS THE BROW JUST SO.

ENJOY EVERY LOOK AND SOUND

THE PRECIOUS LITTLE CHILD SHOWS;

THEN LATER IT CAN BE FOUND

IN YOUR MEMORY….WHEN THE CHILD GOES.

"Children Fly Away"

NO MATTER HOW MUCH YOU WISH THEM TO STAY
TOO SOON YOUR PRECIOUS CHILDREN FLY AWAY.
GONE THEN, WILL BE THE PATTER OF THEIR FEET
THAT COME EACH SLEEPY MORNING, YOU TO MEET.

THEY WILL GROW AND TRAVEL ON DOWN LIFE'S ROAD,
THEY'LL FIND NEW LIVES AND CARRY THEIR OWN LOADS.
BUT DO NOT CRY! FORBID THYSELF TO WEEP!
FOR GOD PUT HIS LITTLE LAMBS IN YOUR KEEP!

LIKE YOU THEY'RE HIS; YOU HAVE THE TENDER YEARS!
YOU HAVE THE MOST PRECIOUS TIMES; SHED NO TEARS!
THE CHILD'S BIRTH….A MIRACLE YOU HAVE KNOWN:
YOUR SWEET CHILD; FROM BIRTH GOD HAS LOANED!

"Children have I See Ears"

OUR CHILDREN LEARN THROUGH THEIR "I SEE YEARS." THEY
MOLD THEIR ADULT LIVES FROM LESSSONS LEARNED.
THE SECRET OF TEACHING LITTLE "I SEE EARS;" IS
SHOWING FROM OUR ACTIONS MORE THAN WORDS!

CHILDREN ARE GROWING, LEARNING SMALL ADULTS;
EVER GROWING, EVER STRIVING TO ACHIEVE.
CONFUSION ONLY HOLDS BACK THEIR GROWING UP. THEY
NEED TO KNOW WHAT'S BEST FOR THEM TO TRY TO BE.

WHAT DO YOUR CHILDREN LEARN FROM YOU EACH DAY?
WHEN THEY ARE LOUD DO YOU CALMLY SAY; "QUIET?"
OR INSTEAD, WITH AN EVEN LOUDER VOICE; "SCREAM HUSH."
DO LITTLE "I SEE EARS" LEARN WRONG OR RIGHT?

IF YOU SCREAMED, THE SCARY LESSON YOU TAUGHT LITTLE "I SEE EARS;"
WAS: THE BIG AND TOUGH MEAN PARENTS CAN DO WHAT CHILDREN
CANNOT! CONCLUSION: NOT WRONG IF YOU'RE BIG ENOUGH!

A CHILD GROWS AND LEARNS TO MATURE BY CHOICE; "I
SEE EARS" MUST LEARN 'MIDST MUCH CONFUSION.
TO SET STANDARDS OF LIFE FROM THE "PARENT VOICE;"
ON WHAT'S SEEN AND HEARD PENDS THE DECISION!

CHILDREN LEARN AS YOU DO, NOT AS YOU SAY! THEY
SHADOW ALL YOUR ACTIONS ONE BY ONE.

I SEE EARS" ARE YOUR SILENT STUDENTS EACH DAY! LEARN
TO DO YOURSELF WHAT YOU ASK FROM ONE!

"Children, I'm Growing Older"

I'M GROWING OLDER GIRLS, I'M 'OFT WEARY AND TIRED;

THOUGH I STILL HAVE MUCH TO DO BEFORE I "RETIRE."

(BUT I WANT YOU TO KNOW)

I NEARLY BURST WITH PRIDE THINKING OF YOUR ACHEIVEMENTS.

YOU HAVE OVERCOME HURDLES, DID WONDERS ON YOUR OWN!

YOU EACH ARE INDEPENDENT AND HAVE TALENTS.

YOU HAVE ACOMPLISHED SO MUCH, SINCE YOU HAVE BEEN GROWN!

NO MOTHER COULD ASK FOR SWEETER, KINDER, GIVING,

ADULTS THAN WHAT EACH ONE OF YOU HAVE NOW BECOME!

AT TIMES, ALONE; EACH OF YOU HAS MADE A LIVING.

EACH OF YOU ARE WONDERFUL MOTHERS ON YOUR OWN!

YOU, YOUR CHILDREN AND YOUR GRANDCHILDREN HAVE BEEN

MY GREATEST BLESSINGS OTHER THAN MY SALVATION!

I AM BLESSED WITH SUCH A LARGE FAMILY, AND THEN

I THINK OF WHEN I WAS A TEEN: ONLY JUST "ONE"

MY LIFE IS FULL, YOU'RE THE FAMILY I WANTED.

YOU GIRLS HAVE BEEN MY HAPPINESS AND BEEN MY JOY!

I HAVE THE HAPPINESS I ALWAYS LOOKED FOR; HUNTED.

I FINALLY FOUND; HAPPINESS IS LOVE: LOVE….JOY!

"Christmas 1971"

THESE ARE THE GOOD TIMES WHEN WE STOP TO HELP EACH OTHER

NO MATTER WHO OR WHERE, WHAT RACE OR COLOR.

NOT TIME TO MAKE A CHRISMAS GIFT, HELP A FRIEND SEW A DRESS,

NOT ENOUGH BILL MONEY, BUT HAPPY WITH LESS!

IT DOESN'T MATTER. A LITTLE LESS CAN NOT MATTER.

WHAT'S IMPORTANT IS THAT WE TOOK THE TIME TO BE TOGETHER.

THESE ARE THE GOOD TIMES, THE POOR TIMES, MINE AND YOUR TIMES.

PERHAPS SANTA GOES TOO MUCH IN DEBT; WE HAVE GOOD TIMES.

'TIS GREAT TO SEE THE CHILDREN OPEN UP THEIR PRECIOUS GIFTS.

IT COST DEAR, LIFE IS SO I FEAR, BUT OH WHAT A LIFT!

IT DOESN'T MATTER, A LITTLE LESS CAN NOT MATTER.

WE'LL ALWAYS REMEMBER THE TIMES WE HAD TOGETHER!

THESE ARE THE GOOD TIMES, TIMES WE THINK OF ONE ANOTHER.

GIVE OUR GIFTS, MAKE BASKETS FOR THE ONES SO MUCH POORER.

THE HAPPY FACE OF THAT LITTLE GIRL…'TWAS ONLY A TOY.

ONE TOY WE GAVE, WAS SO MUCH JOY TO THAT ONE LITTLE BOY.

AND IT DID NOT MATTER TO HIM, HAVING LITTLE DID NOT MATTER:

HIS FAMILY POOR, JUST ONE TOY, HE COULDN'T HAVE BEEN GLADDER.

HE REJOICED IN WHAT HE HAD, AND THAT HIS FAMILY WAS TOGETHER!

"Climb 'Till Your Dreams Come True"

OFTEN YOUR TASKS WILL BE MANY AND MORE
THAN YOU THINK YOU CAN DO.

OFTEN THE ROAD WIL BE RUGGED, AND THE
HILLS UNSURMOUNTABLE TOO!

BUT ALWAYS REMEMBER, THE HILLS AHEAD
ARE NEVER AS STEEP AS THEY SEEM,

AND WITH FAITH IN YOUR HEART START UPWARD;
CLIMB 'TILL YOU REACH THAT DREAM!

FOR NOTHING IN LIFE THAT IS WORTHY, IS EVER EASY TO ACHIEVE:

IF YOU HAVE THE COURAGE TO TRY IT, AND THE FAITH TO BELIEVE!

FOR FAITH IS A FORCE MUCH GREATER THAN
KNOWLEDGE OR POWER, OR SKILL:

AND MANY DEFEATS TURN TO TRIUMPH WHEN
YOU TRUST GOD'S WISDOM AND WILL!

FAITH IS THE MOVER OF MOUNTAINS, THERE
IS NOTHING GOD CANNOT DO!

SO START WITH FAITH IN YOUR HEART, AND
CLIMB 'TILL YOUR DREAMS COME TRUE!

"Come Back"

TO MOM,

IT REALLY BOTHERS ME FOR YOU TO NOT BE AROUND
DURBIN CHURCH THESE DAYS.
FOR EVERYONE IS MISSING THE ONE WHO GAVE BIRTH AND
THE ONE WHO RAISED
THIS DAUGHTER OF YOURS THEY SO 'OFT AND SO HIGHLY
HONOR AND PRAISE.

'TIS KNOWN THE LORD IS ALONE RESPONSIBLE FOR
LOVE AND ALL THAT'S GOOD:
YET ALSO, IT'S KNOWN THAT TO BE KIND IS NATURAL WHEN
TAUGHT ONE FROM CHILDHOOD!
YOU'VE BEEN AWAY FOR SO VERY LONG, THEY KNOW NOT
KINDNESS AS THEY SHOULD;
FOR I COULD NEVER BE AS KIND AS MY TREACHER, HAS O'ER
THE YEARS, SHOWN:
NOR SMILE SO SWEETLY AS YOU CAN SMILE TO LET LOVE
TO OTHERS BE KNOWN!
COME BACK; FOR IF NOW SOME WARMTH IS HERE, I KNOW THE
COOLNESS CAME ONCE YOU WERE GONE!

"Coming Through the Clouds"

SUDDENLY WE WILL HEAR A PIERCING SOUND;

ANGEL GABRIELS' HORN WILL ECHO THROUGHOUT EARTH

ANNOUNCING THE GREATEST EVER OF ALL GREAT SHOWS.

THIS SHOW WILL BE REAL AND FOR ONES RE-BIRTHED!

THOSE RE-BIRTHED IN CHRIST WILL HEAR AND SEE

JESUS IN ALL HIS MIGHT AND GLORY LIGHT UP THE SKY!

A 'MIDST HIS ANGELS AND CHERUBIM, AS THEY SING;

IN ROBES WHITER THAN THE CLOUDS, BRIGHTER THAN THE SKY!

IN ALL POWER AND IN ALL AWESOMENESS HE'LL COME!

HE WILL RAISE US BACK UP WITH HIM TO STREETS OF GOLD

"FOR HE IS COMING TO TAKE ALL OF HIS CHILDREN HOME

JUST AS TOLD IN THE BIBLE, VERY LONG AGO!

"Daddy"

THERE IS NO OTHER WORD

IN ANY LANGUAGE HEARD

THAT MEANS MORE THAN MY DADDY'S!

IF WARBLED BY A BIRD

NO SWEETER SONG IS HEARD

THAN ONE SUNG BY MY DADDY!

THERE IS NO OTHER SMILE

WHEN TRUDGING O'ER THE MILES

PROUD AS ONE OF MY DADDY'S!

TRUE LOVE CAN TURN ONE BLIND

YET THE EYE STILL NOT FIND

A MAN, FINE AS, MY DADDY!

"Daughters" (Each of Four)

TAKE A LOOK AROUND YOUR PRECIOUS REALM OF HOME:

YOU LEARNED FROM ME TO CHERISH AS YOUR OWN.

NOTE THINGS I'VE GIVEN YOU FROM TIME TO TIME'

WISHING YOU TO HAVE SOMETHING PERSONAL OF MINE!

IN YOUR MIRROR SEE THAT SWEET, BEAUTIFUL FACE?

GLIMPSES OF ME ARE HIDDEN THERE FOR YOU TO SPOT AND CHASE!

LOOK AT OUR CHILDREN DAUGHTER, YOU WILL SEE THERE,

TRACES OF ME IN PERSONALITY OR FACE.

LOOK INTO YOUR HEART, SEEK THE DEPTHS INSIDE;

FIND THE LOVE I GAVE YOU, WITH MY ARMS OPEN WIDE!

REACH DEEPLY INTO THE WISDOM HALLS OF YOUR MIND

AND FIND PLANTED THERE; LITTLE WISDOM SEEDS OF MINE.

NOW OPEN ONE MORE DOOR, PEER INTO YOUR SOUL;

AT GOODNESS I CULTIVAED, FOR YOU TO GROW'

THEN, EMBRACE THE SAVIOR, WHO LIVES THERE WITHIN;

TAKE COMEFORT KNOWING I'LL GO TO HEAVEN WITH HIM!

I'LL ONLY GO HOME TO HEAVEN LITTLE GIRLS;

THERE'LL BE A VERY LARGE PART OF ME IN YOUR WORLD!

DRAW COMFORT FROM THE SAVIOR, LIVING IN YOUR HEART;

THEN SOMEDAY YOU WILL JOIN ME THERE, NEVER TO PART!

"Daughters Mine"

DAUGHTERS ARE FOR CUDDLING AND TEACHING "PRETTY PLEASE!
DAUGHTERS ARE FOR BOUNCING ON THEIR DADDIES KNEES.

DAUGHTERS ARE FOR TELLING; "PRETTY IS AS PRETTY DOES."
DAUGHTERS ARE FOR BEING PRECIOUS AND SMOTHERING WITH LOVE!

DAUGHTERS ARE FOR HELPING MOTHERS
WHEN THEY'RE BIG ENOUGH TO.
DAUGHTERS ARE FOR TEACHING TO BE LITTLE
LADIES THROUGH AND THROUGH.

DAUGHTERS TOO SOON HAVE THEIR OWN FAMILIES,
THEN THEIR CHILDREN ARE GROWN;
THEN GRANDCHILDREN ARE A GREAT BLESSING,
DAUGHTERS SHARE WITH THEIR MOTHERS SOME!

BUT IT GOES ON; GRANDCHILDREN GROW UP, AND
YOU'RE A GREAT GRAND-MOTHER NOW.
THE PRIDE IN YOUR DAUGHTERS WHEN YOU SEE
WHAT THEY BECOME IS JUST "WOW!"

TO SEE THEIR ACCOMPLISHMENTS AND MANY
HURDLES THEY HAVE CLEARED
GIVES ME SO MUCH PRIDE AND PLEASURE I
FIND A TEAR IN MY EYE THERE!

DAUGHTERS ARE SO VERY PLEASING, ALL IN
ALL, JUST WHAT MOTHERS NEED;
FOR MOTHERS LOVE THINGS BRIGHT AND
BEAUTIFUL, DAUGHTERS ARE THESE!

"Dear Little One"

FROM THE GARDENS OF HEAVEN, GOD SURELY CHOSE,

THE WHITE OF THE LILLIES, THE PINK OF THE ROSE;

THE RED OF THE TULIP, THE GOLDENROD FAIR,

FOR YOUR SKIN, PINK CHEEKS; YOUR LIPS AND HAIR!

OUT OF PINK BLOSSOMS, HE FASHIONED YOUR EARS.

THEN GOD TOOK THE DAISY, ITS' PETALS SO SWEET;

FOR YOUR FINGERS AND TOES: AND YOU WERE COMPLETE!

AND THE ANGELS WERE SMILING THE DAY OF YOUR BIRTH;

AT A BEAUTIFUL BABY: "YOU!" GOD'S GIFT TO THE EARTH!

"Denise"

LIFE IS FUNNY IN ITS TWISTS AND TURNS;

TRIALS AND CHANGES THAT MAKE HEARTS YEARN.

BUT ALL THINGS ARE FOR REASONS DENISE,

A PATTERN THAT EVER CHANGES WITHOUT CEASE!

LIVES ARE DIRECTED IN PATHS THEY MUST TROD,

SOME BELIEVE BY FATE, OTHERS BELIEVE BY GOD!

YET THE CHANGE IS SET, IN LIFE AND IN TIME;

WHILE YOU ARE LEFT WITH; THE REASON, TO FIND!

WHAT LIES AHEAD; JOY, SADDNESS, YOU CHOOSE,

FOR IN LIFES CHOICES HEARTS WIN OR THEY LOSE!

YOUR PATH HAS CHANGED, MUCH WAITS AHEAD;

A FRONTIER FOR YOU TO ENJOY OR DREAD.

DEAR, YOUR PATH WILL CROSS MANY OTHERS NOW.

CHOOSE WELL FRIENDS YOU ACCEPT WITH A SILENT VOW;

FOR WITHIN THESE CROSSINGS OF PATHS IT SEEMS

LOVE, JOY; HAPPINESS OR SORROW IS SURELY DEEMED!

I WISH YOU WELL AS 'LONG LIFES' PATH YOU GO

MAY YOU IN LOVE, HAPPINESS AND KNOWLEDGE GROW!

"High School Theme, Shakespear Style"

"DIM DARK THOUGHTS"

LOOSE ME FROM YOUR HOLD, DIM DARK THOUGHTS,

WITHIN YOUR GATES MY PAIN IS UNDULY WROUGHT.

WHY MUST YOU HAUNT ME? LET ME BE FREE!

LET ME LIVE MY LIFE WITHOUT THE CHAINS OF THEE!

LET ME ALONE, YOU DEMONS FROM BLACKEST HELL!

YOUR HOLD IS WORSE THAN THE TOLL OF DEATH'S BELL.

HAPPINESS IS MINE! MINE YOU HEAR, AWAY!

AWAY WITH YOU! LET MY LIFE BE SWEET AND GAY!

LET ME TASTE THE DEW DROPS OF A LOVE TRUE.

HOW I LONG FOR THE ODOR OF A HEAVENLY ATMOSPHERE.

MY LONGINGS HAVE SO LONG BEEN HELD, BOUND,

AND JUST AS I THOUGHT AN ESCAPE I'D FOUIND;

YOUR DARK FINGERS CLUTCHED, PULLED AND TORE

UNTIL FINALLY I WAS CAUGHT AS OF YORE!

AND OH THE PAIN, THE DEEP LIFE-SEEKING PAIN;

HAS FOUND MY HEART, I MUST DIE AGAIN!

FORGET ABOUT FRIGHTENING

THOUGHTS AND THINGS;

YOU CAN NOT ENDURE THE SONGS I SING!

I'LL SING MERRILY OF HAPPINESS ALL THE DAY.

"TILL FINALLY YOU DIE WITH THE PAST, I'LL BE GAY!

"Dory"

YOU KNOW, GOD MAKES LITTLE GREEN APPLES,

HAPPY HEARTS AND WONDERFUL MIRACLES.

HE MAKES BIG PINK CLOUDS WITH WHITE LACING,

PUPPY DOGS AND WAVES WITH WHITE ICING!

HE GAVE YOU LIFE, A CHUCKLING BABY;

A COOING, GROWING, LITTLE LADY.

IT'S BEEN ROUGH, THOUGH HE'S CARRIED YOU THROUGH.

LIFE'S BEEN HARD, BUT HE'S WATCHED OVER YOU!

HE'LL GIVE YOU A LIFE; HAPPY, COZY;

TURN THINGS HUNKY DORY, RIGHT ROSY!

SO JUST QUIT CHASIN' THAT BIG RAINBOW,

YOU AINT GONNA FIND NO POT OF GOLD!

QUIT SEEKING PEACE IN A DREAM COME TRUE

AND JUST LET GOD BRING PEACE RIGHT TO YOU:

'CAUSE GOD DOES MAKE LITTLE GREEN APPLES

AND YOU KNOW HE DOES MAKE MIRACLES!

SO LET HIM BRING ALL YOUR DREAMS ALIVE,

GIVE YOU THE HAPPIEST LIFE EARTH-WIDE!

"Dream on Dreamer"

DREAM ON LITTLE DREAMER, DREAM ON.

DREAMS HAVE KKEPT YOU GOING THIS LONG!

THE WAVE OF HOPE, T HE THOUGHT ANEW;

HAVE CALMED, HAVE FRESERVED YOU!

DREAM ON MIND, NEVER LOSE YOUR DREAM!

WITHOUT YOUR DREAMS; LIFE, HOPELESS WOULD SEEM!

MIND, DO NOT DWELL ON LIFES' HARDSHIPS NOW

REST, RELAX; DREAMER, DREAM ON FOR AWHILE!

"Each Child is a Sunbeam"

EACH CHILD IS A SUNBEAM
SENT FROM HEAVEN ABOVE.
NOURISH EACH LITTLE SEED
AND COVER IT WITH LOVE!

THEY ARE FEW YOU RECEIVE,
SWADDLE EACH ONE WITH CARE.
CUDDLE YOUR SUNBEAM SWEET
LET IT SHINE EVERYWHERE!

THEY WILL SHINE EVERYWHERE
TO EVERYONE THEY MEET!
IF EACH OF US DID THIS
THE WHOLE WORLD WOULD TURN SWEET!

"Emma"

I NEVER COULD QUITE PINPOINT THE REASON,
BUT YOU REMAIN AS SUNSHINE IN ANY SEASON.

THE YEARS TUMBLE AND QUICKLY SLIP AWAY,
BUT YOUR LAUGHTER IS THE SAME AS YESTERDAY.

AS THE DAWN AWAITS THE COMING OF THE SUN
YOU AWAIT TO SEE THE BRIGHT SIDE WHEN THERE IS NONE!

WHEN YOU SEE SOMETHING THAT NEEDS DONE, YOU JUST DO IT.
AND IF YOU SEE SOMEWHERE A FAULT, YOU ALWAYS PERSUE IT.

TO A FRIEND YOU'RE ALWAYS READY TO LEND A HELPING HAND;
OR GIVE A CRITICAL OPINION IF THE SITUATION DEMANDS!

BUT EVER IN HEART, IN FRIENDSHIP, IN LIFE; YOU REMAIN TRUE
AND IT'S A PLEASURE TO HAVE A FRIEND SUCH AS YOU!

"Flowers"

PUT TINY LITTLE SEEDS
IN HOLES IN THE GROUND.
THEN ALL THEY NEED
WILL COME AROUND.

RAIN WILL SHOWER DOWN
AND GIVE THEM A SUP.
THE LITLE BITTY SEEDS
WILL SWELL ALL UP.

POP! POP! POP!
FLOWERS WI LL COME UP!

"Forgive Me Lord"

FORGIVE ME LORD, FOR DEEDS PAST AND GONE.

FORGIVE ME LORD, FOR THINGS I HAVE DONE WRONG.

FORGIVE ME LORD FOR THE PATH I WALKED.

FORGIVE ME LORD FOR THE WAY I TALKED.

FORGIVE ME LORD FOR WHAT I'VE BEEN.

FORGIVE ME LORD FOR ALL MY SINS.

I REALIZE I HAVE BEEN WRONG IN THE PAST.

LORD I SEE THE BLESSED LIGHT AT LAST!

"Freedom! Justice!"

"FREEDOM;" I CRY! "FREEDOM;" "LET US BE FREE!"
OH FREEDOM; HOW CHAINED YOU NOW HAVE BECOME!
WE CAN'T SPANK OUR CHILDREN OVER OUR KNEES.
IF YOUR WAYS DIFFER FROM THE NORM YOU'RE DUMB.

"FREEDOM;" I CRY! "FREEDOM;" "LET US BE FREE!"
GOD DID NOT MAKE MEN TO ALL BE THE SAME?
I AM DIFFERENT...AND I WILL BE ME!
I AM NOT A NUMBER, I HAVE A NAME!

"JUSTICE;" I CRY! "JUSTICE;" TREAT ALL MEN FAIR!
FELONS SPEND MORE JAIL TIME THAN ONES WHO KILL!
INNOCENTS MUST LIE TO SPEND LESS JAIL TIME; UN-FAIR!
MUST PLEAD QUILTY: COP A PLEA: "LESS TIME DEAL."

"Friend of Mine"

I'VE WRITTEN MANY POEMS TO FRIENDS FAR AND WIDE
BUT THERE'S NOT BEEN ANOTHER STICK SO CLOSE BY MY SIDE.

DAILY YOU ARE THERE IF I HAVE A QUESTION FOR YOU
OR IF I JUST NEED A FRIEND TO SAY HELLO TO.

WHATEVER I ASK OF YOU IS NEVER EVER TOO MUCH.
WHERE ELSE COULD I FIND A CLOSE FRIEND AS SUCH?

A FRIEND IS A GIFT OF GOD; WELL YOU CAME WITH A BOW,
FOR YOUR FRIENDSHIP IS SO SPECIAL, WARM AND A-GLOW!

AND THAT EXTRA GIVING; BECAUSE YOU LOVE, IS AN ART.
I THANK YOU SO, BECAUSE YOU GIVE FROM YOUR HEART!

"Friendship"

TO EMMA ON HER BIRTHDAY:

MY FRIENDSHIP ASKS NOT THAT YOU BE AS I AM
NOR DOES IT SAY CONFIDE YOUR SECRETS TO ME.

I WOULD BE MY OWN FRIEND IF I WANTED A FRIED AS I AM,
NOR CAN I ASK YOUR SECRETS, WHEN MY OWN I KEEP CLAM.

MY FRIENDSHIP ACCEPTS YOU JUST AS YOU ARE,
I DON'T BASE OPINIONS ON WHAT I HEAR A-FAR.

YOU ARE MY FRIEND BECAUSEE MY HEART SMILED
AND YOUR HEART OPENED WIDE.

AND WHEN TWO HEARTS SMILE AND SAY HELLO
A FRIENDSHIP IS BORN ANEW.

TO ME, FRIENDSHIP COMES FROM WHAT I FEEL INSIDE,
AND WHEN WE MET SOMEHOW I FELT A FRIEND IN YOU.

"Friend True"

ARE YOU A FRIEND, TRUE TO THE END,

OR DO YOU CARE FOR ME,

JUST A LITTLE MORE?

DO YOU EVER WANT TO BE

THE ONE I'M WAITING FOR?

"Getting Older"

SPRING BLOSSOMS OF BEAUTY: SO FRESH! SO

NEW! THEY BRING MISTY TEARS

I NOW FIND SPRINGS SWEETNESS: SWEETER

THAN THE ONES IN YESTER-YEARS!

OH SWEET CLOYING SUMMER: LONG HOT DAYS,

THEN A COOL, SWEET NIGHTS BREEZE;

THAT WAFTS HALLS OF MY MIND, WITH CHILDHOOD SUMMER MEMORIES!

FALL HUES ARE FABULOUS: REDS AND BROWNS

DEEPER, THE GOLDS, GOLDER!

COOL MORNINGS WHITE FROST: THE HARVEST

THEN HOLIDAYS IN ORDER!

THE SILENT WINTER WHITE: NOISY HUSTLE AND

BUSTLE, WITH CHRISTMAS NEAR;

NOW ANTICIPATED; NO FEAR OF COLD, NO LONGER DREAR!

ONCE A FLOWER PETAL GAVE MY EYE OY, AND WARMED MY YOUNG HEART;

BUT NOW WITH JOY SERENE: I SELFISHLY

CHERISH EACH SOFT CURVED SPOT!

THE BUTTERFLY FLUTTERING: I WISH I COULD

KEEP THE BLACK THE GOLD!

EACH SINGLE FLUTTER IS A LASTING SIGHT, PRECIOUS TO BEHOLD!

AH THE INNOCENT BABE: SUCH A MIRACLE OF WONDER REAL!

TO TOUCH, HOLD, AND SEE; JOY SUBLIME, AGED SENSES, TO SEE TO FEEL!

I'M GETTING OLDER; TRUE, BUT GOD HAS

BLESSINGS FOR OUR AGED PLIGHTS:

WHAT SOME CALL SECOND CHILDHOOD, I KNOW

IS "CHILDHOODS NEW, FIRST SIGHT!

"Give Me God, Liberty and Love"

I MAY NOT ALWAYS HAVE HAD THE BEST OF EVERYTHING:

I MAY HAVE SOMETIMES BEEN SAD, BUT YET COULD SING!

IT TAKES ONLY ONE SMILE TO CHASE THE BLUES AWAY,

OR ONE SONG TO BRING HAPPINESSS TO ONE WHOLE DAY!

FIRST OF ALL IN THIS UNIVERSE WE NEED OUR LIVING GOD!

WHOM WITHOUT THERE WOULD BE ONLY EMPTY SPACE!

WITH COMPASSION HE COMFORTS US, THE ONE TRUE GOD!

HE LOVES EACH AND EVERYONE OF THE HUMAN RACE!

SECOND IN THIS WIDE, WIDE WORLD WE NEED LIBERTY,

SOMETHING TO LIVE FOR, FREEDOM OF WORDS AND LOVE;

A RIGHT TO LIVE FREE, HAPPY, A REASON TO BE!

WE NEED FREEDOM TO BE PURE, CLEAN, LIKE A WHITE DOVE.

THIRDLY, WE NEED LOVE AND WE NEED A HOPE THAT'S DEAR:

SOMEONE TO CARE FOR, TO LOVE, AND SOMEONE WHO ALSO CARES!

WE NEED A LOVED ONE, A SWEETHEART, ONE ALWAYS NEAR

WHOM ONES' THOUGHTS, ONES' HEART, ONES' LIFE SHARES.

YES, GIVE ME GOD, LIBERTY AND LOVE; AND I WILL BE FREE,

HAPPY, JOYFUL, SO GLAD THAT I'M LIVING TODAY!

I'LL HAVE NO PROBLEMS, OF LONLINESS I'LL BE FREE.

GIVE EVERYONE GOD, LIBERTY AND LOVE, I SILENTLY PRAY!!

"Glenda"

YOU ARE MY PRECIOUS LITTLE MAY FLOWER
UNSELFISH, THOUGHTFUL, LOVING, BEAUTIFUL.
AS SWEET AND FRESH AS A SPRING MORNING BREEZE
AS CHEERFUL AND GAY AS BIRDS IN THE TREES.

YOU ARE MY PALE YELLOW MAY FLOWER GIFT
WHO CAME ONE SPRING DAY TO GIVE OTHERS BLISS!
DELICATE, YET STRONG AND STURDY INSIDE;
WITH SO MUCH TALENT. WALK IN BEAUTY; PRIDE!

WATCHING A SPRING FLOWER GROW AND BLOOM
HAS BEEN THE SWEETEST PURE PLEASURE, A BOON.
YOU'VE GIVEN ME SWEET GIFTS AT LENGTH.
A GENTLE FLOWER GIVING TO OTHERS STRENGTH!

LOVE GIVES STRENGTH TO PEOPLE LIKE RAIN SHOWERS,
WARMTH AND SUNSHINE STRENGTHENS FLOWERS!
YOU SHARE THAT STRENGTH WITH OTHERS OFTEN,
EVEN PASSING BY AS YOU JUST GO OUT WALKING!

YOU HAVE GIVEN SO MUCH TO ME ALWAYS;
YOU GIVE AND YOU GIVE IN SO MANY WAYS.
THE MANY GIFTS GIVEN; AND YOUR SWEET, KIND WAYS,
HAVE BRIGHTENED AND COMFORTED ALL MY DAYS!

"God Cares for Mothers"

GOD SEES EACH TEAR A MOTHER CRIES
COUNTS ALL A MOTHERS WORRIED SIGHS
HEARS EACH MOTHERS HOPEFUL PRAYER:
FOR OUR JESUS TOO, HAD A MOTHER HERE!

GOD CHERISHES A MOTHERS SPECIAL WAYS
THE ALL KNOWING SPECIAL WORDS SHE SAYS
FOREVER HOLDING HER HEART OPEN WIDE;
NURTURING THE CHILDREN THAT ARE HER PRIDE!

"God Created Mother"

GOD CREATED EVERYTHING

BUT TO SHOW HIS LOVE

AND GIVE US BEAUTY

HE CREATED YOU

MOTHER!

"Gods' Gift of Beauty"

BURST FORTH CROCUS, TULIP, DAFFODILL
AND TINY WILD SPRING FLOWERS DEEP IN THE FIELD.
OPEN YOUR PETALS TOWARD HEAVEN ABOVE
AGAIN 'TIS TIME TO SHOUT GODS' BEAUTY AND LOVE!

ONLY OUR FATHER COLD CREATE THIS DREAM;
THE BIRTH OF LIFE AROUND US, WE CALL SPRING!
WHO COULD DENY THE LOVE OF THE MIGHTY ONE,
WHO GIVETH BEAUTY, LIFE AND GAVE US HIS SON?

BURST FORTH BEAUTY, WE AWAIT REBIRTH
OF LIFE TO WINTER-FORSAKEN EARTH!
BURST FORTH AND SHOW THE LOVE IN GODS' PLAN;
BEAUTIFUL LIFE, GODS; GIFT OF BEAUTY TO MAN!

"God's Little House"

I WALKED INTO CHURCH TIRED AND WEARY
AND MY HEART WAS TROUBLING ME SO.
I SAW GODS' HOUSE WAS WARM AND CHEERY
AND 'ROUND ME CHRISTIAN FACES DID GLOW.

WHEN I LIFTED MY FACE ONE GAVE A SMILE
THEN ANOTHER CHEERFULLY SAID; "HELLO:"
SO THUS I DID REST IN GODS HOUSE FOR AWHILE.
I FELT HIS WARMTH, HEARD HIS WORD: THEN DID GO.

I THANK GOD FOR THE COMFORT OF HIS FAMILY HOME,
FOR THE FELLOWSHIP WITH HIS CHRISTIANS 'ROUND.
FOR THE CHEER, THE WARMTH, THE; "HELLO," THE SMILES SHOWN;
FOR THE OPEN HEARTS OF PEOPLE TOGETHER, "HEAVEN BOUND!"

"God's Love in You"

OH HOW THE LORD LOVETH A CHILDS PURE HEART!

BORN BETWEEN TWO BROTHERS: ONE YEAR APART.

ONE WAS OLDER, ONE YOUNGER, ME; BETWEEN.

WHEN I WAS STILL A YOUNG INNOCENT THING;

I PRAYED FOR A SISTER WITH ALL MY MIGHT!

HIS HEART SOFTENED TO ME THAT NIGHT.

WHEN I WAS EIGHT YOU CAME, CRYING LOUD!

THE GOOD LORD LISTENED TO THIS LITTLE CHILD.

THE WAR HAD LEFT AN EVIL STENCH BEHIND

THAT LOOMED OVER OUR FAMILY ALWAYS.

DAD HAD BEEN TRAINED TO FIGHT ON THE FRONT LINE!

HIS HEART HARDENED; TAUGHT TO KILL EV=RY DAY.

THEY TRAINED THOSE THEY THOUGHT TO BE TROUBLE; TOUGH!

NOT KOWING THEIR TRAINING WAS WAY TOO ROUGH!

BUT YOUR PRESENCE BROUGHT OUT LOVE BROUGHT BACK GOOD.

GOD SENT YOU, LOVES YOU; WILL CARE FOR YOU!

"Gods' Tree"

RUSTLE ON LEAVES OF THE BIG OAK TREE; TALK
TO THE WIND, GROW RESTLESS LIKE ME!
LEAVES YOU BELONG TO THE BRANCHES; THEY
BELONG TO THE TREE, ROOTED IN CLAY.
OAK TREE YOUR ROOTS GROW DEEP, NARROW; YOU'RE
THERE TO STAY, TODAY AND TOMORROW.
THROUGH SEASONS YOU WILL STAND TALL AND GROW.
YOU'LL REACH OUT, BUT NEVER CAN YOU GO.
IN SPRING YOU WILL BUD, NEW LEAVES WILL GROW;
BUT RESTLESS THEY WILL TOSS TO AND FRO.
IN THE SUMMER YOU'LL GROW TIRED AND HOT, TO
FIND A PLACE COOL, SWEET, YOU CANNOT.
THEN FALL WILL COME, YOU WILL LOSE YOUR LEAVES.
YOUR VERY SOUL WILL GRIEVE AT FALL'S PLOT!
WINTER WILL COME WITH COLD SNOW AND ICE.
YOU ARE STUCK HERE IN THIS COLD,
COLD LAND!
STUCK HERE TOGETHER ARE YOU AND I, AND
PLACED HERE ON PURPOSE BY GODS' HAND!
OUR ROOTS ARE DEEP, WE CAN NEVER STRAY; BUT
WHISPER TO GOD, FOR PATIENCE PRAY.
OH RESTLESS LEAVES, RUSTLE ON AND ON; HERE
YOU MUST STAY 'TILL YOUR WORK IS DONE!

"Gods' Will"

WHEN ONE EMBARKS UPON GODS' WILL

OFT' HE ASKS AT THE FOOT OF THE HILL:

"LORD WHAT COULD I OR SHOULD I DO?"....

NOT SEEING GODS' PATHWAY SHINING THRU!

THE HILL LOOKS RUGGED AND OH SO TALL.

DO YOU THINK GOD WOULD LET HIS CHILD FALL?

HE SIMPLY WAITS WITH OUT-STRETCHED HAND

TO SHOW YOU THE "GREATEST MASTER PLAN."

IT TAKES BUT ONE TURN OF YOUR HEART....

AND HE WIL LEAD YOU PAST EACH HARD PART!

YOU ONLY NEED REACH FOR HIS HAND!

BEFORE YOUR BIRTH HE WORKED OUT THE PLAN!

BLIND...WE SEEK SUCCESS AND HAPPINESS:

OUR TALENT LYING IN A BABES' NEST....

WHIL'ST GOD WAITS PATIENTLY ABOVE

TO MAKE OUR TALENT GROW....WITH HIS LOVE!

WE HAVE WINGS TO FLY UP THAT HILL....

OR LIE THERE IN OUR NEST, A BABE STILL.

WE CAN BLINDLY HOPE FOR SUCCESS

OR USE HIS PLAN FOR HAPPINESS!

"Gods' Wind"

GODS' WIND SAILS DOWN THRU THE SOFT GRASSY LAWN

AS IF STRETCHING IN EARLY MORN TO YAWN.

SHE GROWS SPEED TO MOVE THRU BUSHES AND TREES.

WITH HER SECOND WIND SHE RUSTLES THE LEAVES.

THEN SHE LIGHTLY COASTS, TO FACE HER DAY. SHE

PLAYS COYLY...WHISPERING ON HER WAY.

SHE HAS SEEN EVERYTHING AS YOU MUST KNOW,

FOR THERE IS NOWHERE SHE DOES NOT GO!

IT MUST BE MYSTERIOUS SECRETS KNOWN SHE TELLS

THE LEAVES, THEY SHIMMER AND SHAKE SO.

THEN SHE WHIPS AWAY IN GUSTS, FAST AND SMART...

TO SEE THE ANT HIDING 'NEATH THE TREES BARK

SHE FINDS THE MOST SECRET THINGS OF THE

HEART. SHE KNOWS THE HID NEST OF THE

MEADOW LARK!

LEAVES, HIDDEN IN CREVICES VERY DEEP.....WAKE AT

HER VISIT AND THEN THEY CAN'T SLEEP.

SHE FINDS A YOUNG GIRL AND WHIPS UP HER HAIR.

OH THE FUN SHE HAS, PLAYING WITH THE AIR.

SHE SOFTLY BLOWS A BUTTERFLYS' WINGS DRY

TO LET IT FLY AGAIN UP TO THE SKY.

ALL OF HER DEEDS AND PLAY JUST IN ONE DAY COULD

NOT BE TOLD E'RE ONE GREW OLD AND GRAY!

"God will Comfort Thee"

I WISH I COULD STAY A LONGER WHILE
BUT WHEN I'M AWAY I WILL SEND A SMILE…
YOU MUST CATCH IT, TO COMFORT BRING
AND LISTEN TO THE SONG THE BLUE BIRDS SING.

AND LET IT TELL YOU THAT COMFORT WILL
COME FROM UP ABOVE EVEN GREATER STILL.
IF ONLY YOU WILL LET IT BE
GOD WILL FULLY COMFORT THEE!

"Gold Coin"

THIS LITTLE PIECE OF GOLD
IS GOOD ALL O'ER THE WORLD.
COLLECT ALL THEM YOU CAN,
THEY'RE POWER IN YOUR HAND.

THEY SAY; "IN GOD WE TRUST;"
THE "ONE" COMPLETELY JUST.
MAN'S MONEY CHANGES WORTH'
MAN OFT' FAILS US; OFT' HURTS.

GOD AND GOLD ARE BOTH TRUE;
NEITHER WILL FAIL FOR YOU.
ONE FOR HEAVEN; ONE…EARTH.
SAVE YOUR GOLD, PUT GOD FIRST!

BE WISE, GENTLE, BE KIND;
GREAT OF HEART, AND OF MIND.
TRUST IN GOD, SAVE YOUR GOLD…..
TRAVEL WELL DOWN LIFES' ROAD!

"Grandfather"

GRANDFATHER DEAR, HOW CAN YOU SEEM SO NEAR?
THO' YOU PASSED AWAY LAST YEAR; YOU SEEM HERE.

OUR FATHER MUST HAVE SOME UNKNOWN SECRET WAY
OF RETURNING YOUR SPIRIT, TO ME ON A BLUE DAY.

FOR WHEN I BECOME LONESOME I THINK OF YOU.
IT SEEMS LIKE MY SECRET THOUGHTS; YOU KNOW TOO.

THE NEW BABE LYING THERE IN HER TINY LITTLE BED,
UNKNOWN TO YOU WHEN AWAY BY OUR FATHER YOU WERE LED:

I KNOW YOU SMILE AT HER AND THINK SHE IS JUST SWELL
AND MY HOW YOUR PATIENCE SHE PRACTICES SO WELL!

I CAN FEEL YOU PACING THE ROOM VERY NEAR,
THO' I KNOW YOU'RE IN HEAVEN, HEAVEN MUST BE CLOSE HERE.

YOUR PRESENCE IS SUCH A COMFORT TO ME GRANDFATHER DEAR,
THO' YOU LEFT US LAST YEAR, IT'S NICE TO HAVE YOU VISIT HERE!

"Grandmother"

WHEN I FEEL HELPLESS AND ASK THE LORD FOR COURAGE TO CARRY ON,

'OFT I REMEMBER GRANDMOTHER, FOR I'M DOING AS SHE HAS DONE.

WHEN LIVES AROUND ME ARE TROUBLED

AND I ASK HELP THRU' GODS' SON;

AGAIN I THINK, AS OFTEN; "THIS I KNOW MY GRANDMOTHER HAS DONE!"

WHEN I'M FILLED WITH FAITH IN THE LORD, OH

SO SURE THINGS WILL TURN OUT RIGHT;

I FIND I'M FOLLOWING MY GRANDMOTHERS' EXAMPLE, NO DOUBT!

THE LORD GIVES ME COURAGE, LIGHTENS MY

BURDENS, SHOWS ME FAITH WILL WIN!

"LORD BLESS MY LITTLE GRANDMOTHER, FOR

ALWAYSS GUIDING ME AWAY FROM SIN!

BLESS HER LORD, FOR ALL THE TRARS SHE'S BRUSHED AWAY'

BLESS HER DEAR LORD FOR ENCOURAGING US THROUGH DARK DAYS.

BLESS HER WEAKENED BODY, FOR SHE WORKED

HARD TENDING OTHERS NEEDS!

BLESS HER LORD FOR PLANTING SEEDS OF LOVE AND FAITH FOR THEE.

BLESS HER FOR TEACHING US CHILDREN THE BIBLES' WAY!

BLESS HER FOR EVER BEING READY TO LISTEN OR PRAY.

BLESS HER LORD FOR ALL SHE'S GIVEN TO OTHERS AND TO ME!

BLESS HER ESPECIALLY LORD FOR HER LOVING LIFE'S RECEIPE:

PRAYER EACH DAY: AS MANY ASPOSSIBLE

FAITH: YOU CAN'T ADD ENOUGH

HOPE: YOU MAY HAVE TO SEARCH

LOVE AND CHARITY: MIX THEM WELL, ONE WILL

NOT RISE WITHOUT THE OTHER

TEN COMMANDMENTS: LEAVE NONE OUT, NEEVER FORGET ONE!

WITH THIS RECEIPE MAY YOU GROW IN LOVE, IN

HONOR AND IN STATURE WITH MAN AND GOD!

"Grandmother I Miss You"

'TIS A SHAME GRANDMOTHERS DON'T STAY HERE.
THEY OWN A PLACE IN OUR HEART SO DEAR!

THEY DON'T THINK THE SAME AND HAVE 'ODD' WAYS'
THEY LINK OUR LIVES TO THE 'REAL' OLD DAYS!

BUT THERE COMES A TIME GOD CALLS THEM HOME:
IT'S SAD FOR US WHEN TIME COMES: THEY GO ON!

BUT THERE IS NO PAIN IN HEAVEN THERE,
JUST REST FOR THE LABORERS DOWN HERE!

SHE LABORED SINCE AGE SEVEN DOWN HERE.
SHE NEEDS THE REST.....I SHOULD DRY THAT TEAR!

"Grannies Hymn"

GRANDMA BENTLEY WOKE UP DREAMING
AND SINGING THIS SONG; IN 1973.

"I'M GOING TO HEAV'N!" (CHORUS)
I'M GOING TO HEAV'N, DON'T YOU WANT TO GO TOO?
EVERYBODY OUGHT TO WANT TO GO TO HEAV'N, HEAV'N!!
EVERYBODY OUGHT TO WANT TO GO SEE
OUR LORD AND SAVIOR! (REPEAT)
EVERYBODY OUGHT TO WANT TO GO TO HEAV'N. HEAV'N!

"WHAT GLORY IT IS JUST TO THINK ABOUT
GOING TO SEE OUR LOVED ONES."
'JUST THINK WHAT IT WILL BE WHERN WE SEE
OUR FRIENDS AND LOVED ONES!'

"I DREAM'T I SAW MY HUSBAND STANDING THERE
IN HIS OLD HAT AND GRAY-BROWN COAT.
MY DEAR LORD WAS WAITING NEIGH THERE TO
GIVE US ALL A BRAND NEW CLOAK!

I'VE GROWN OLD AND TIRED, MY HAIR IS GRAY.
I'VE BEEN READY FOR SOME TIME TO GO.
BUT SOMEHOW I'VE JUST BEEN HANGIN' ON FOR
SOMETHING I'VE JUST GOTTA' KNOW!

BEFORE I LEAVE THIS OLD WORLD OF SORROW,

HARDSHIP, TOIL AND FEAR;

WILL YOU ANSWER ME ALL MY LITTLE CHILDREN;

WILL YOU MEET ME UP THERE?

WILL YOU PUT YOUR HAND IN JESUS' STRONG

HAND, WALK WITH HIM ALL THE WAY?

E'RE I REST ON MY SWEET SAVIORS' BOSOM, TELL

ME; WILL YOU MEET ME THERE SOMEDAY?

SHE SAID IN HER DREAMS SHE SANG WITH THE VOICE OF AN

ANGE! SHE ADDED; "I NEVER HAD A GOOD SINGIN' VOICE, BUT IN

MY DREAM I SANG SO PRETTY HONEY, JUST LIKE A' ANGEL."

"SHE ASKED ME TO WRITE IT UP FOR HER BEDCAUSE I

WAS GOOD AT WRITING. I TOOK NOTES AND WROTE

IS AS CLOSE AS I COULD TO HER WORDS. 1975

"Granny"

EACH NIGHT AS I PREPARE TO LIE DOWN,

IN MY BUREAU I SEE GRANNIES COTTON GOWN.

MOTHER PASSED IT DOWN TO ME;

DID SHE KNOW IT'D BRING, SUCH SWEET MEMORY?

GRANNIES SWEET WRINKLED FACE APPEARS

IN MY MIND. MEMORIES OF GOOD OLD YEARS

COME SLOWLY BACK AGAIN

TO WARM MY HEART, FOR HER LOVE STILL SPEAKS SO PLAIN!

I THINK OF HER LOVE, HER FAITH; HER STRENGTH;

THE MAHY LITTLE THINGS SHE EXPLAINED IN LENGTH.

THE TIME SHE TOOK FOR EVERY NEED,

HOW LOVINGLY; "DON'T FORGET TO PRAY;" SH'D PLEAD!

THE LOVE, THE LAUGHTER, WARMTH OF HER HOME

WILL EVER FOLLOW THE PATH THAT I ROAM!

I LOOK FORWARD TO THE DAY,

"UP THERE; "I'LL BE WAITING HONEY," SHE WILL SAY!

1979

"Guardian Angels

I'M GOING TO SLEEP AND I KNOW I'M SAFE.

ANGELS ARE WATCHING FROM THAT HIGH PLACE!

ANGELS IN HEAVEN WILL TAKE CARE OF ME....

NO BETTER GUARDS COULD THERE EVER BE.

THEY WATCH OVER ME DAY AND NIGHT

TO SEE TO IT THAT EVERYTHING GOES ALRIGHT.

THEY'RE WATCHING AND I HAVE NO FEAR,

OF ANY KIND OF DANGER LURKING NEAR.

SO INTO SLUMBER I WILL SLOWLY SINK

ANGELS ARE WATCHING I WILL THINK,

AND SOON I WILL DOZE AND SLEEP,

INTO DEEP SAFE PEACEFUL SLEEP.

KNOWING GOD'S ANGELS WATCH OVER ME

SAFE AND HAPPY I WILL BE.

GOODNIGHT WORLD, I HOPE YOU TOO

HAVE ANGELS IN HEAVEN WATCHING OVER YOU!

"Happy Anniversary Peggy"

IT'S BEEN A LONG ROAD, BUT YOU'VE GOT TO THIRTY

FEEL FREE TO HAVE A GOOD TIME; GET ALL PURTY.

CELEBRATE, LAUGH, AND ENJOY, BUT THEN REMEMBER

ALL THE GOOD TIMES, SWEET WORDS AND WARM DECEMBERS.

LIFE IS WAY TOO SHORT, MAKE THIS DAY SWEET

AND BE HAPPY ALL OVER FROM YOUR HEAD TO YOUR FEET!

HAPPY ANNIVERSARY PEGGY AND JERRY!

"Happy Mothers Day"

(TO THE LADIES AT CHURDH)

I SALUTE THE LADIES WHO HAVE LED THE LITTLE CHILDREN HERE.
BEEN AN EXAMPLE AND BLESSING TO US FOR SO MANY YEARS.

YES, YOU! THE ONES WHO HAVE HELPED WITH PRAYERS AND TEARS
AND LOVED AND LED EVEN ONES WHO ARE NOW GRANDMOTHERS HERE!

HAPPY MOATHERS DAY TO ALL YOUNG, OLD OR IN BETWEEN
BUT A SPECIAL SALUTE TO THOSE THE MOST YEARS HAVE SEEN!

BLESS YOU FOR SMILES YOU'VE GIVEN THE CHILDREN O'ER THE YEARS.
BLESS YOU FOR THE PRAYERS SENT FOR OTHERS CARE AND TEARS!

SOME OF YOUR FACES I'VE SEEN HERE SINCE I WAS A TINY TOT!
OTHERS HAVE COME ALONG AND JOINED OUR HAPPY LOT!

I REMEMBER YOUR SWEET FACES WHEN I WAS A CHILD; LOST AND 'LONE
AND KNOW ONLY THROUGH THE FATHER
COULD YOU SO SWEETER GROWN!

FOR AS I LOOK AROUND THE PEWS, YOURS ARE THE LOVLIEST FACES,

SOFTENED O'ER THE YEARS BY LOVE AND

PRAYER FOR OTHERS AND FOR ME!

IF MY SIGHT BE CLOUDED WITH LOVE, THOUGH I THINK THIS NOT SO;

LORD KEEP IT CLOUDED FOR THESE ASE THE

SWEETEST FACES I'LL EVER KNOW!

"Happy Wedding Day"

AS PRECIOUS AND BEAUTIFUL AS YOUR WEDDING DAY;

MAY YOUR LIFE STAY AS BEAUTIFUL ALWAYS.

MAY EACH DAY THAT COMES CELEBRATE YOUR SWEET LOVE,

MAY YOUR LOVE BE BLESSED BY THE LORD; UP ABOVE.

IN UNITY AS ONE, START A LONG LOVELY LIFE.

MAY YOU HAVE LITTLE SADDNESS AND LOTS LESS STRIFE!

YOUNG LOVE IS ONE OF THE SWEETEST5 GIFTS ON EARTH,

AS WAS THE MIRACLE FROM GOD OF YOUR BIRTH!

NEVER FORGET THE SWEET LOVE OF YOUR WEDDING DAY

MAY IT LAST THE SAME 'TIL YOU'RE GROW OLD AND GRAY!

"Harvest for the Lord"

REAP A GOOD HARVEST FOR THE LORD.

SING OUT HIS NAME TO THE WORLD!

SHOUT HIS PRAISES FROM HILL TO HILL

AND PRAY THAT EVERYONE WILL DO HIS WILL!

TEACH THE CHILDEN OF HIS LOVE:

OF NOAHS' ARK AND OF THE DOVE.

RING THE CHIMES IN THE STEEPLE,

TEACH HIS WORD TO ALL THE PEOPLE!

WAKE THE TOWN AND SING AND SHOUT

TELL EVERYONE WHAT THE BIBLE IS ABOUT!

SING AND SHOUT AND PRAISE HIS NAME,

SOON OTHERS WILL DO THE SAME!

TELL HIS STORY ALL AROUND....

TELL OF THE WONDERFUL SAVIOUR YOU FOUND!

"Have Hope"

DO NOT REGRET PAST TROUBLE AND WOES.

THEY ARE AS A VINE THROUGHOUT YOUR LIFETIME.

IF YOU HAD NOT SUFFERED SOMEWHAT BEFORE,

WHEN TIMES GET WORSE; COULD YOU SUFFER MORE?

BE AS A HUGE OAK, WITH ROOTS FIRM AND TRUE,

THEN THE TROUBLING VINE WILL SEEM SMALL TO YOU!

STAND TALL AND LET GOD YOUR FOUNDATION BE!

HE'LL NOT LET YOUR TROUBLES GROW TOO HEAVY FOR THEE.

WHEN WE REACH HEAVEN, THAT BEAUTIFUL, GOLDEN, SOMEWHERE

WE SHALL FORGET ALL THE TROUBLE AND SICKNESS WE HAD HERE!

"Have You Met Him?"

DOWN YOUR LIFE'S LONG, RUGGED HIGHWAY,

DO YOUR FEET TRUDGE ALONE EACH DAY?

AT NIGHT WHEN YOU LAY DOWN YOUR HEAD

DO YOUR THOUGHTS TURN TO LONESOME PAIN AHEAD?

THEN YOU MUST NOT HAVE MET HIM,

OR LEFT HIM BACK ALONG THE WAY.

FOR HE MAKES LIFES' JOURNEY PLEASANT

AND A TALK WITH HIM GIVES HOPE FOR THE DAY!

WON'T YOU MEET MY GOOD FRIEND CHRIST JESUS:

HE WAITS ALONG THE WAY TO MEET EACH OF US.

OUR OTHER DEAR ONES COULD LET US DOWN OR PASS ON;

MAKING US WALK LIFES' ROAD UNCOMFORTED AND ALONE.

OH YOU MUST MEET MY GOOD FRIEND CHRIST JESUS!

HE'LL NEVER EVER LEAVE YOU EVEN AT LIFES' END!

THOUGH ALL OTHERS FAIL OR FORSAKE US,

JESUS WILL REMAIN OUR COMFORTER AND OUR FRIEND!

THOUGH OUR BEST FRIEND EVER, HE'S MUCH MORE.

HE OVERCAME DEATH AND OVER ACROSS THE SHORE;

HE'S BUILDING US A HEAVENLY HOME AND TAKING CARE

THAT ALL WILL BE JUST PERFECT WHEN WE ARRIVE THERE

"Hectic!"

MY IT WAS A HECTIC DAY,

AS OFTEN GOES A MOTHERS' WAY.

PROBLEMS GALORE

A CHILD SICK, WORRY, FRET

A STORM, RAINY AND WET

DAD WORKING OVER-TIME;

HOW 'OFT I ASK "WHAT MORE?

THANK YOU LORD FOR EVEN TODAY

THOUGH HECTIC SUCH WAS THE WAY

YET WHEN EVENING CAME

WE WERE ALL CLOSE AND WARM:

TELLING STORIES, READING YOUR WORD

THE CHILDRENS' LAUGHTEER HEARD

DAD GOT IN SAFE AND SOUND

YES, WE WEATHE RED THE STORM!

IN BEAUTY GOES THE CLOSE OF DAY

THOUGHTS OF WHAT THE CHILDREN SAY

PROBLEMS ALL DISAPPEAR

AND OH HOW WELCOME; REST.

THANK YOU LORD, THANK YOU AGAIN

FOR ENDING TODAY AS YOU PLANNED

WITH THE SUN SHINNING THROUGH!

"He'll Be With You"

LOVED ONES NEVER GO AWAY
THEY REMAIN IN YOUR HEART
EVER WITH YOU NIGHT AND DAY;
FOR OF YOU' THEY ARE A PART!

HE'LL BE WITH YOU NOW FOREVER;
LOVE SURPASSES LIFE YOU KNOW!
NO! HE IS NOT GONE FOREVER;
HIS LOVE GOES WHERE E'RE YOU GO!

IN HEAVEN YOU WILL MEET AGAIN
AND WALK THE STREEETS OF PURE GOLD.
HE JUST MOVED TO A HIGHER PLANE
HIS LOVE GOES WHERE E'RE YOU GO!

"Hello World"

"HELLO WORLD AND HOW ARE YOU TODAY?"

"JUST THE SAME I SEE, AS YESTERDAY."

"OH ME?" "WELL I GUESS I'M DOING FINE;

I'LL KNOW I GUESS BUT IT TAKES TIME."

"I'VE GOT THE BLUES WORLD, I DON'T KNOW WHY;

BUT I'M NOT GOING TO LAY HERE AND CRY."

"NO, NO, THAT'S NOT FOR ME TO DO:

I'M GLAD WORLD, YOU THINK SO TOO."

"BUT TELL ME, DO YOU REALLY AGREE?"

"WORLD YOU KNOW YOU CAN'T FOOL ME."

"WHY, WHEN YOU GET THE BLUES IT STARTS TO RAIN,

AND I KNOW THEN WORLD, YOU'RE CRYING IN VAIN."

"WHEN YOUR HEART GROWS COLD IT BEGINS TO SNOW,

AND WHEN YOU'RE RESTLESS, HOW THE WIND DOTH BLOW;

BUT WHEN YOU'RE HAPPY, HOW THE SUN DOTH SHINE."

I KNOW THEN DEAR WORLD, EVERYTHING IS JUST FINE!"

"High on Happiness"

LET'S GET HIGH ON HAPPINESS

HIGH ON HAPPINESS

BACK TO THE GOOD LIFE

LET'S GET DOWN, DOWN; DOWN.

COUNT YOUR BLESSSINGS ONE BY ONE

FIRST: WHAT JESUS DONE.

HE DIED ON THE CROSS

OF HIS FREE WILL: "FOR US"

TWO: COUNT THE BEAUTY GIVEN

IT CAME FROM HEAVEN

WONDERS YOU CAN SEE,

CREATED FOR YOU, ME!

LET'S GET HIGH ON HAPPINESS

BACK TO THE GOOD LIFE

LET'S GET DOWN, DOWN, DOWN!

"His Gift of Life"

JUDAS BETRAYED: "JESUS OF NAZARETH" PRAYED. JUDAS,

WITH A KISS OF DEATH; JESUS' IDENTITY GAVE!

THEY SPAT ON AND SMOTE THE SAVIOR WITH NO SIN: PUT A

THORNY CROWN ON HIM WOVEN BY THE ROMAN MEN.

THEY FOUND A PURPLE ROBE FOR HIM TO PUT ON, CHIDING:

THEN BID ON THE ROBE, HOLY BLOOD HAD FELL UPON.

PILATE FOUND NO FAULT, WHEREAS JESUS SHOULD DIE; BUT

SCOURGED HIM JUST BEFORE THE MULTITUDE CRIED CRUCIFY!"

THE CAT-O-NINE TAILS CUT WITH EVERY WHELT! HOLY BLOOD

SPLATTERED: BUT FOR US HE ENDURED PAIN HE FELT.

THUS; HE STROVE CRUEL GOLGOTHAS' STEEP TRAIL. DEATHLY

WEAK, NEATH A HEAVY CROSS. ALAS; OUR JESUS FELL.

SO, SIMON BORE ITS' WEIGHT FOR HIM ON UP TO CALVARY.

JESUS CRIED; "FATHER, THEY KNOW NOT WHAT THEY DO."

SOLDIERS DROVE SPIKES IN BOTH HIS HANDS AND FEET. SUDDENLY

JERKING UP THE CROSS; RAW SPLINTERS SANK IN DEEP!

HIS VITAL BLOOD SEEPED AWAY. COULD IT BE LONG? MUSCLE

AND SOCKETS WERE SEPERATED FROM JESUS' BONE!

HOURS PASSED. HIS SUFFERANCE SUFFICIENT, HE CRIED; "IT IS

FINISHED." "FATHER I COMMEND MY SPIRIT;" AND DIED!

BUT FROM AN UNTOUCHED; SEALED, GUARDED GRAVE HE CAME:

SEEN IN BOTH SPIRIT AND FLESH; SCARS PROVING S HOLY NAME!

HIS BLOOD PAID THE COST FOR ALL MANS' SINS YOU SEE. HE

AWAITS, HE CALLS; "BELIEVE, I PREPARE A PLACE FOR THEE!"

"Holy Bible"

HOLY BIBLE, BOOK OF LOVE, WORDS OF THE FATHER ABOVE

THY PAGES HELD IN MY HAND; THY MOST PRECIOUS GIFT TO MAN

PASSED ON THRU THE AG

S BY THY CHOSEN SAGES

FILL THE SOULS EVERY NEED; IF MEN WILL ONLY, ONLY READ!

THROUGH THY PAGES SO DEAR ARE WORDS SOUND AND CLEAR

OF THY INSTRUCTION AND LOVE, AND HOPE TO JOIN THEE ABOVE.

THY WORDS SHOW HAPPINESS TRUE THRU A LIFE SO PURE AND NEW;

PEACE, NOTHING EARTHLY CAN EXPRESS;

LOVE THAT WILL EVER, EVER LAST.

MEN DAILY SEEK AND NEVER FIND SUCCESS AND HAPPINESS OF MIND.

FOR THEY NEVER THINK TO LOOK IN THE

HOLY BIBLE; MOST PRECIOUS BOOK!

THE LIGHT IS THERE TO PERCEIVE IF THEY ONLY READ AND BELIEVE!

"Hope"

LOOKING BACK SUCH A SHORT TIME AGO I FIND

OUT JUST HOW MUCH I DIDN'T KNOW.

I SEE NOW JUST HOW SILLY, HOW IMMATURE I DID

SEEM, LIVING FOR SUCH AN IMPOSSIBLE DREAM.

I'M SO GLAD TODAY I CAN SEE THINGS AS THEY ARE; AND I AM ME!

OH THE PEACE THAT COMES WITH BEING MATURE,

IT'S NEXT BEST TO HEAVEN I'M QUITE SURE.

NOW I MUST GO ON, DO THINGS I HAVE TO DO. AT

TIMES I'LL BE HAPPY, AT TIMES I'LL BE BLUE.

BUT LIFE IS NOT FULL OF SUGAR AND CREAM NO

MATTER HOW YOU MAY PRETEND OR DREAM.

I'M HAPPY NOW JUST BEING ME ALONE! LIVING

THE LIFE OF A PERSON WHO'S GROWN.

IT IS QUITE PLEASING JUST TO KNOW WHO I AM, PLACES I WISH TO GO;

WHAT I WANT OF LIFE AND WILL TO GET IT, I'LL

MAKE THAT TOP SHELF, YOU CAN BET IT!

BECAUSE I PLAN TO LIVE MY LIFE TO PLEASE ME, TO

HELP OTHERS ALSO PERHAPS IF IT CAN BE!

"Hope for Your Hard Struggle"

I WISH TO BE OF HELP TO YOU, A GRACIOUS LADY; YET I AM WEAK.

WITH THE LORDS' HELP, I'LL TRY THE ONLY

WAY I KNOW HOW; PEN AND INK!

THROUGH YOUR WEB OF LIFE, YOU'VE HELPED MEND OTHERS VIEWS.

YOUR HAPPY BUSY WEAVINGIS FULL OF BEAUTIFUL LOVING HUES!

SO NOW, WHILE YOUR WEB ENDUREDS ROUGH WEATHER, DON'T DESPAIR!

MANY PRAYERS ARE WITH YOU AND JESUS' BOSOM IS ALWAYS THERE.

ACCCEPT WHAT YOU CANNOT CHANGE, WHEN YOU ARE WEARY PRAY

PEACE BE STILL. JESUS WILL CALM THE ROUGH WEATHER EACH DAY!

THOUGH WEAVING LIFES' WEB IS TIRESOME AND HARD TO ENDURE

YOU NEED NOT CARRY SO MUCH BURDEN ON YOUR HEART SO PURE!

CEASE TO STRUGGLE, TO KEEP EACH FIBER IN TACT; STRIVE NO MORE.

LET JESUS MEND YOUR HEALTH AND YOUR HEART THAT ACHES SORE!

HE IS THE "GREAT COMFORTER" AND CAN HELP

AS NO OTHER FRIEND CAN DO.

JESUS IS THE "GREAT PHYSICIAN" HE'LL SEE THE MEDICINE HELPS YSOU!

REST WEARY "DAUGHTER." WEARY "SISTER,"

WEARY MOTHER," PEACE BE STILL!"

LET JESUS TAKE EACH THOUGHT, ERACH QUESTION, EACH LITTLE PILL;

UNTIL YOU HAVE NO WORRY OR EVER WONDER "WHAT SHOULD I DO."

EVEN MORE AS THE "PHYSCIAN," HE'LL SEE THE MEDICINE HELPS YOU.

JESUS IS OUR PHYSIAN AND OUR BEST FRIEND INDEED;

RELAX, DEAR LOVING JEANNE, LET HIM ATTEND EVERY NEED!

"Hopes and Dreams"

YOU MAY BREAK MY HEART, YOU MY DISSAPPOINT ME TOO
BUT ANOTHER BEAUTIFUL DREAM WILL GROW IN PLACE OF YOU.
MY ARMS HAVE ACHED, MY LONELY HEART HAS OFTEN CRIED.
BUT ALWAYS THERE WAS HOPE, THAT'S HOW I HAVE SURVIVED.
I HAVE BEEN THROUGH TORTURE, I HAVE SUFFERED NEAR HELL,
BUT MY HOPES AND MY DREAMS LIE DEEP WITHIN THE WELL.
IN THE DEEPEST WELLS OF MY HEART, OF MY SOUL AND MIND
ARE NEW DREAMS AND NEW HOPES; THIS BODY IS WELL LINED.
NEVER WILL I FALL, NEVER EVER SHALL THIS HEART OF MINE DIE
FOR MY HOPES AND DREAMS ARE A PART OF THE VERY SKY.
MY HOPES AND DREAMS ARE BIGGER FRIEND THAN YOU AND I.
THEY ARE SO BIG THEY'LL LIVE ON TILL THAT GREAT "BY AND BY."
THE WORLD IS MADE OF PEOPLES HOPES AND PEOPLES DREAMS
MY HOPE LIES IN THE HANDS OF THE GREATEST CREATOR OF DREAMS!

"How to be Happy"

I REMEMBER WHEN I WAS BORED, DESPERATE AND ALONE;

NOW I THANK GOD ALL OF THAT IS PAST AND GONE.

FOR NOW THERE ARE NOT ENOUGH HOURS IN THE DAY

TO DO ALL THAT NEEDS DONE, HELP OTHERS AND PRAY.

SOMETIMES MY PERSONAL WORK I MUST LET GO UNDONE,

FOR GODS; WORK COMES FIRST AND SOULS NEED WON!

THEN TOO I KNOW, WORK FOR THE ONE WHO IS MOST HIGH

PRECEEDS EARTHLY WORK AND PLEASES JESUS WHO'S NEIGH.

BOREDOM, DESPERATION, LONLINESS ARE FAR FROM ME NOW

I HAVE PEACE, BUBBLING JOY; MAY I TELL YOU HOW?

SEEK THE LORD, IF LOST LET THE SAVIOR SAVE YOU;

AND IF SAVED, YET LONELY, BORED; PRAY VERY SOON.

THE SECRET IS TO PRAY EACH AND EVERY SINGLE DAY

THAT GOD WILL LEAD YOUR LIFE, YOUR WILL. JUST SAY

FATHER TAKE ME, USE ME, THY WILL BE DONE NOW;

THEN HE WILL PUT YOU TO USE. FRIEND THIS ALONE IS HOW

TO BE HAPPY AND BUSY IN THE LORD, AND HE IN YOU.

HE'LL HAVE YOU STUDY HIS WORD, FOR HIM WORK AND DO.

YOUR BOREDOM, DESPERATION AND LONLINESS WILL BE O'ER

AND YOU'LL FINALLY KNOW THE WORK YOU'RE PUT HERE FOR!

"Humble Me Lord

LORD BLESS ME AS I GIVE IN TO THEE
AND MAKE ME WHAT I OUIGHT TO BE.
I NEED THY STRENTO LOSE OLD WAYS,
LET THIS BE DONE. GTH YO CARRY ON.
LORD HUMBLE ME IN THE WAY NOW,
WHAT SHALL I DO LORD? TEACH ME HOW.
THY WAYS I WISH TO LEARN TO KNOW.
HELP ME DEAR LORD, THY LOVE TO SHOW.

LORD GRANT THAT I NO TIME SHALL WASTE
LEARNING THY LOVE, LEARNING THY GRACE.
I CANNOT DO THY WORK UNTIL
LORD, I COMPLETELY LEARN YOUR WILL!

LORD SUFFER ME THY WILL TO LEARN
AND THEN TO YOU, OTHERS HELP TURN.
WHEN HEAVENS' GATE OPENS THAT DAY
LET ME KNOW I'VE HELPED SHOW THY WAY!

"I Am a Child of Jeses'"

I AM A CHILD OF JESUS'.

FOREVERE LET ME BE!

I AM A CHILD OF JESUS'

THROUGH A CHILDS EYES I SEE!

SOME MAY THINK ME SIMPLE

TO TAKE LIFE DAY BY DAY;

BUT 'HE' KEEPS TOMORROW

AND PLANS IT BEST HIS WAY!

A CHILD SEES TRUTH THAT'STHERE!

HIS HEART KNOWS RIGHT FROM WRONG!

GOD SHOWS THEM SIMPLE TRUTH,

GUIDES THEIR LIVES, LEADS THEM ON!

WHEN CHILDREN HAVE A GOAL

IT NEVER LEAVES THEIR MIND!

THEY WON'T REST 'TILL IT'S DONE:

THEY KNOW NO QUITTING TIME!

TRUTH THE BIBLE TELLS THEM,

WITH THEIR HEARTS THEY BELIEVE!

THEY CAN FEEL TRUTH AND LOVE!

OH BLESSED LORD, KEEP ME A CHILD OF THEE!

"I Choose to Smile"

I'M HAPPY WITH LIFE, FORGETTING ALL STRIFE;
'TILL DISRUPTIONS MAKE ME BLINK!

THEN SORROW I SPY, PROBLEMS EVER LIE
SO SULLENLY 'NEATH THE BRINK!

MY SINGING DOTH CEASE, AS MY BROW DOTH CREASE;
INTO PAIN AND DESPAIR I SINK!

HAPPY I WOULD BE, CHEERFUL AND CAREFREE;
IF NEVER I STOPPED TO THINK

BUT THEN ONCE AGAIN I BRACE UP AND GRIN
AND AT LIFES' FOLLIES I WINK

FOR I CHOOSE TO SMILE AND IGNORE LIFES' VILE
UNHAPPINESSS
THAT I DRINK!

WITH LAUGHTER I'LL DROWN, THE PAIN I PUSH DOWN
E'ER ALWAYS TIED TO ITS' LINK

"I'd Long to Be"

"I'D LONG TO BE AS FREE AS THE WIND,
AS WILD AS A THUNDER STORM.

I LONG TO FLY, PURE AND WHITE AS A DOVE
AND TO FLOAT LIKE A SOFT WHITE FEATHER.

I WOULD LIKE TO BE ABLE TO BLEND
INTO A DIFFERENT FORM.

I WOUILD LIKE TO BE A SWEET WORD OF LOVE
BUT MOST OF ALL I'D RATHER

JUST BE A PAIR OF LIPS,
FOR YOU TO KISS!

"If I Couldn't See"

I WONDER WHAT LIFE WOULD BE

AND HOW I WOULD FEEL

IF I COULDN'T SEE.

HOW'D I FEEL TO HEAR THE WHISPER OF THE TREES,

THE CHIRPING OF THE BIRDS, THE SPLASHING OF A WAVE;

THE BUZZING OF THE BEES?

I'D HEAR THE LEAVES RUSTLE,

THE BIRDS WARBLE;

THE SPLASHING WAVE

AND THE BUZZING OF THE BEE.

I'D NEVER SEE THE SHAPE OF A LEAF,

COLORS OF THE TINY BIRDS;

THE CURLED WAVE FROM THE ROARING SEA SPLASH,

OR THE TINY BLACK AND YELLOW BEE!

I WOULD SADLY SIGH AND THINK ON ALL OF THESE!

"If I Were"

"IF I WERE A BUTTERFLY LIFE WOULD SIMPLE BE,
I'D FLIT HERE AND FLIT THERE, SO BEAUTIFUL AND FREE.

IF I WERE A DAISY I'D DRINK IN SUN AND RAIN;
AND ANSWER QUESTIONS, 'LOVED OR NOT' FOR LOVERS VAIN!

IF A BUTTERFLY, I'D POP OUT IN EARLY SPRING
WITH A PROMISE OF WARMTH TO COME AND SONGS TO SING!

IF I WERE A LILY FAIR WITH MUCH BEAUTY BLESSED,
I'D CARRY THE HONOR TO GRACE A SWEET HEARTS CHEST!

IF I WERE A GRACEFUL SWAN, I'D FLOAT WATERS DEEP'
FOR THE EYE TO SEE ME "AND" MY SHADOW; SO SLEEK!

"I Found My Way"

I WAS LOST IN THIS WICKED, WIDKED WORLD.

DEEP AND DEEPER STILL I WHIRLED!

I WAS A LOST, LONELY, WANDERING SHEEP.

OFTEN, YES, VERY OFTEN 1 DID WEEP.

HIS COMMANDMENTS I WAS BREAKING ONE BY

ONE. IN SIN, THOUGHT I WAS HAVING FUN!

OH HOW, HOW WRONG CAN A LOST SOUL BE;

WHEN GODS' LIGHT IS S0 SIMPLE TO SEE?

I SARCHED AND SEARCHED FOR HAPPINESS; WANTING

GODS' WONDERFUL BLESSEDNESS.

BUT WOE, I KNEW NOT WHAT I SOUGHT FOR I

WAS LOST IN SIN WITH A CLOSED DOOR!

THEN WITH THE HELP OF A WOMAN DEAR TO

ME; GOD OPENED THE DOOR, I CAN SEE!

NOW I PRAISE GOD AND SING OUT HIS NAME; HE

TOOK AWAY ALL MY SIN AND SHAME!

I AM NO LONGER LOST IN SIN AND WOE; FOR

THEIR IS A SAVIOUR FOR US, I KNOW.

HE SAVED ME FROM SIN AND THE BURNING FIRE;

I'M HAPPY8 WITH LOVE AND PRAYER!

I HAVE LOVE AND WONDERFUL PEACE TODAY, I LIE NOT IN SIN; I PRAY!

I PRAY THAT MILLIONS OF PEOPLE EVERY DAY; LOST

AND WANDERING, FIND THEIR WAY:

LEARN TO LOVE AND PRAISE GOD AS I DO,

FOR HE IS SAVIOR OF ME AND YOU!

THE LEAST I CAN DO IS WORK FOR HIM EACH

DAY, FOR HE TOOK ALL MY SINS AWAY!

WORK FOR GOD AND LOVE AND PRAISE HIM, OTHER

LOST SHEEP EILL BE SAVED FROM SIN!

THEY WILL ALSO LOVE AND WORK AS WE DO, THEN

OTHERS WILL BE SAVED FROM SIN TOO!

"I Have Heard"

THE YOUNGER GENERATION WANTS A WORLD OF LOVE

THEY WANT TO RID THE WORLD OF WAR AND OF HATE:

I HAVE HEARD;

THEY NO LONGER WANT TO BE HANDLED WITH KID GLOVES,

AND THEY ARE SICK AND TIRED OF THE LIE, THE FAKE:

I HAVE HEARD;

THEY SEEK TRUTH, FOR WHAT IS HAPPENING, WHAT IS REAL.

THEY DETEST PAREENTS PRETENDING PERFECT LIFE:

I HAVE HEARD;

THAT ALL: WHICH IS GOOD, PURE AND TRUE, THEY WANT TO FEEL,

BUT THAT WHICH IS NOT THEY HAVE ALL HAD THEIR FILL:

I HAVE HEARD;

THE BIBLE HOLDS THE PUREST LOVE, TRUTH AND WISDOM.

THIS BEING SO; SEEK LOVE AND KNOWLEDGE FROM ONE:

"IF YOU ARE SINCERE."

YOU LEARN THE BOOK WELL, THAT YOU MAY PASS IT ON DOWN.

THIS YOU FAILED TO RECEIVE; NOW PASS IT AROUND:

"FOR IT IS YOUR HERITAGE!"

"I Know Whom I have Believed"

(A SONG WITH THIS NAME WAS WRITTEN LONG AGO) CHORUS: FOR I KNOW WHOM I HAVE BELIEVED AND AM PERSUADED THAT HE IS ABLE TO TAKE THAT WHICH I'VE COMMITTED UNTO HIM AGAINST THAT DAY! OH NOW I NEED THY STRENGTH THEREOF FOR NOW THE WORST BLOW OF MY LIFE HAS COME. I'M WEARY LORD, BUT I MUST GO ON. MY YOUTH AND STRENGTH HAVE EBBED WITH AGE. OTHERS YOU HAVE TAKEN TO HEAVEN LORD, THERE MUST BE A REASON FOR ME TO STAY. WHAT E'RE IT IS LORD I WILL DO. YOUR WILL, I WILL EVER OBEY.

MY HOME HAS FALLEN AROUND ME DOWN HERE, THOUGH YOU HAVE A NEW HOME FOR ME SOMEDAY! THANK YOU LORD FOR CARING FOR ME ALL MY LIFE. WHEN HOPE WAS GONE, YOU CAME ALONG. NOW, IF MY HOME BE BROKEN AND I BE LEFT ALONE, I STILL HAVE LIFE, AND MUST HAVE A MISSION TO FILL, OR LONG AGO YOU WOULD HAVE GATHERED ME HOME.

EASE MY BROKEN HEART NOW LORD, LEND ME STRENGTH TO CARRY ON. THOUGH ALL SEEMS LOST, 'TIS ONLY LOST IN THIS WORLD. I KNOW HEAVEN WILL BE BLISS FOR THIS OLD GIRL! I KNOW NOT HOW I WILL LIVE ON SO LITTLE HERE, I CANNOT WORK AT A JOB SINCE THAT CAR WRECK; BUT I HAVE LIFE, YES, ONCE AGAIN YOU WERE THERE!

YOU NOW HAVE FOUND ME A WONDERFUL GOSPEL CHURCH. WITH MY CHILDREN YOU ARE ANSWERING MY PRAYERS. THE GRANDCHILDREN, ONE BY ONE ARE BEING SAVED; I KNOW THEY WILL HAVE YOU TO RELY ON IN THEIR LIFE AND CAN MEET ME UP IN HEAVEN WITH YOU SOMEDAY.

MANY LITTLE CHILDREN AT CHURCH AND MANY ADULTS
HUNGER FOR GOD'S LOVE, AND ARE IN NEED OF A FRIEND.
OUR LAND HAS BECOME UN-HOLY TO THE POINT OF INSULT;
PEOPLE FEAR TO LIVE WHILE FEARING THE END!
HELP ME TO DO ALL THAT I CAN, NOT MINE BUT YOUR WAY. YOU ARE
EVER THERE, ONLY ON THEE LORD CAN I DEPEND, FOR LOVE AND CARE!
I PRAISE THEE O LORD! AMEN

"I'll See Jesus' Face"

I HAVE A FUNNY FEELING I'M GLAD TO BE HERE.

IT IS SO WONDERFUL WITH MY LORD SO NEAR!

I FEEL A PLEASANT PEACEFULLNESS DEEP IN MY HEART;

LIKE THE SINGING OF A PRETTY MEADOWLARK.

IT IS SO WONDERFUL TO BE HAPPY AND HAVE PEACE!

I KNOW TOMORROW I WILL SEE JESUS' FACE!

"I'm Satisfied Lord"

I'M SATISFIED WITH JUST A COTTAGE BELOW.

YOU'VE GIVEN ME A LITTLE SILVER.

YOU'VE GIVEN ME A LITTLE GOLD,

AND A LOVING HUSBAND;

FOUR CHILDREN TO WATCH GROW,

A CHANCE TO DO MANY THINGSS THAT ARE GOOD

JUST LIKE I ONCE DREAMED IN M Y CHILDHOOD.

YOU HAVE LET ME GIVE TO OTHERS

BEAUTY WORKED WITH MY OWN HANDS:

JUST AS I SAW LONG AGO

IN A LITTLE CHILDS DREAM LAND.

THEN MUCH MORE THAT I HOPED;

SO MANY BLESSINGS, COMFORT WHEN SAD,

JKINSPIRATION WHEN NEEDED LORD

AND JUST WHAT I NEEDED WHEN THINGS WENT BAD.

MOST OF ALL;

FROM A LITTLE FRIGHTENED BABE

WITH LITTLE BEAUTY EVER AROUND,

YOU'VE MADE LIFE BEAUTIFUL AROUND ME

AND ALL MY SINS YOU HAVE FORGAVE!

I PRAISE THEE O' LORD!

"I Remember Girls"

I REMEMBER HOLDING YOU FOR THE FIRST TIME;
CHECKING TO SEE IF YOU HAD ALL YOUR FINGERS AND TOES.
HOW I RELISHED IN YOUR RESEMBLENCES OF MINE:
HOW I SMILED WHEN I FIRST SAW YOUR TWIN TOES!

YOU WERE TINY, SO SOFT; A LITTLE MIRACLE TO ME:
A MINIATURE PERSON; NEW PINK CHEEKS AND ALL NEW PINK SKIN!
YOU WERE SO SWEET AND WONDERFUL TO SEE,
I INSTANTLY FORGOT THE HARD BIRTH PAINS!

OH HOW SWEET THOSE INNOCENT, BABY BLUE EYES.
HOW I CHERISHED THOSE PRETTY PINK BABY CHEEKS!
HOW SWEET, THE AFTER BATH BABY SMELL: OH MY!
BLISS: BABY ASLEEP ON YOUR SHOULDER CHEEK TO CHEEK!

OH THE LIGHT IN YOUR EYE TO SEE A PRETTY THING.
HOW YOU'D GET EXCITED, REACH OUT FOR IT AND LOOK AT ME;
KICKING THOSE TINY CHUBBY LEGS, LOOKING UP, ASKING!
I TICKLED YOU AND SOMETHING ELSE TOOK YOU TO SEE.

"It's All So Near the End"

LIFE IS ALL SO VERY SWEET MY DEAR

AND THE END OF US ALL IS SO VERY NEAR I FEAR.

DO NOT FRET O'ER QUICKSANDS OF THE MIND

NOR THE MANY TROUBLES FOUND OF THE WORLDLY KIND.

BUT ONLY FIND WHERE YOU STAND WITH GOD!

DON'T SEEK THE PASSAGES UNDERNEATH,

BUT LOOK CONSTANTLY UPWARD TOWARD HEAVENS' WREATHS!

ALL THINGS HERE ARE JUST GOOD TO CONFUSE:

BUT GOD HAS PLANS FOR YOU, HE HAS A BETTER USE!

YOU CAN'T UNDO MATTED, TANGLED WEEDS,

FOR THEY WOULD BREAK BEFORE THE END YOU COULD EVER SEE.

LEAVE ALL ELSE AND FOLLOW GOD TODAY

FOR IT IS SO VERY NEAR THE END OF THE WAY.

HE'LL STRAIGHTEN THE TANGLED QUICKSAND MASS;

HE KNOWS THE NUMBER ON EARTH OF EACH BLADE OF GRASS!

"I Walked a Lonely Road"

I WALKED A LONELY ROAD

AND THEN I FOUND A BAG OF GOLD.

I LEFT IT LAY, IT WAS NOT PUT THERE FOR ME.

IT STILL LIES THERE 'NEATH AN OLD OAK TREE.

I WALKED ALONG UNTIL I SAW AFAR,

UP IN TH SKY, A LONELY, LONELY STAR.

ALL AT ONCE THE STAR BEGGAN TO FALL!

FALLING, FALLING, PAST THE MOON AND ALL.

I REACHED OUT TO CATCH IT WHEN IT FELL;

AND IT CAME STRAIGHT INTO MY ARMS!

"Jefffery Bryant"

ONLY SIXTEEN, WATCHING YOU WHEN EMMA WENT TO WORK;

I DID EXACTLY THAT; I WATCHED YOU AND NOTHING ELSE!

I WATCHED EVERY FACIAL EXPRESSION, EVERY LITTLE QUIRK!

WHEN YOU SMILED IN YOUR SLEEP, YOU SAW ANGELS I FELT!

EVERY MOVE YOU MADE WAS A PRECIOUS THING TO ME,

YOU WERE SO SPECIAL, BELONGING TO EMMA AND J;

SHE WAS MY VERY BEST FRIEND FOR LIFE YOU SEE!

YOU SEEMED SUCH A MIRACLE WHEN BORN ONE DAY!

YOUR MOTHER WORLKED AWFULLY HARD, SO DID YOUR DAD.

I DID NOT WORK AT ALL, JUST PLAYED WITH YOU ALL DAY'

SO IT DID NOT TAKE VERY LONG FOR HER TO GET A BIT MAD;

WORKING AND COMING HOME TO WORK, NO TIME TO PLAY.

SOME OF THE WORK I COULD EASILY HAVE DONE, I HAD TIME.

FINALLY SHE ASKED IF I HAD DONE ANYTHING THAT DAY;

I ANSWERED THAT I'D WATCHED YOU ALL THE TIME!

SWEETLY, SHE TOLD ME I COULD HELP OUT SOME EACH DAY.

I TOOK TIME TO LOOK AT HER GOOD; SHE LOOKED SO TIRED.

I REALIZED I SHOULD HAVE BEEN HELPING WITH HOUSE WORK

SO SHE'D HAVE TIME TO REST, TO HOLD YOU, TO GET UNWIRED.

I DID, BUT EACH DAY MISSED JUST WATCHING YOU AS "MY WORK!"

"Jesus' Greatest Miracle"

OUR JESUS, THE WONDERFUL MIRACLES HE WOVE: YET

WOULD NOT SAVE HIMSELF WHEN NAILS THEY DROVE!

HE LET THEM PIERCE HIS HANDS AND FEET: FEET THAT

TROD, HANDS THAT HEALED ONES HE DID MEET!

HE DID NOT SCREAM, HE DID NOT SHOUT; AS HIS

BLOOD AND HIS LIFE FLOWED OUT!

HE CRIED INSTEAD; "FORGIVE THEM, THEY KNOW NOT WHAT THEY DO!"

HE CHOSE TO DIE ON THAT CROSS FOR YOUR SINS, AND MINE TOO!

AND HE DID! HE DIED ON THAT CRO0SS OF A TREE SO

WE COULD GO TO HEAVEN; YES YOU AND ME.

HE KNEW OF SATANS POWER IN THE FUTURE AND IN THE PAST

WOULD BE USED TO THE FULLEST TO HOLD US FAST!

HE KNEW ALL THE MIRACLES HE HAD ALREADY DONE

WERE NOT ENOUGH TO PROVE GOD TO EVERYONE!

BUT TO DIE ON THAT AND FOR GOD TO RAISE HIM FROM

DEATH BACK TO LIFE; WOULD MAKE THE BATTLE; "WON!"

TO SAVE OUR SINS, BLOOD WOULD HAVE TO BE SHED! JESUS WAS

THE LAMB; SACRIFICE FOR THE LIVING AND THE DEAD!

ONLY GOD HAS POWER OVER LIFE AND DEATH YOU KNOW! HE

DID NOT SAVE HIMSELF, HE DIED, GODS' POWER TO SHOW!

JUDGEMENT DAY WILL SURELY COME AND WHAT WILL YOU

CHOOSE? WE WILL BE WITH OUR SWEET JESUS, YOU COME TOO!

"Jesus has Shown Me the Way"

I LOVE JESUS, HE HAS SHOWN ME THE WAY.

HE HAS SHOWN ME THE RIGHT PATH TO FOLLOW.

HE ANSWERS MY PRAYERS WHEN I PRAY.

HE WILL BE WITH ME TODAY AND TOMORROW!

JESUS, PRECIOUS JESUS, I LOVE HIM MORE EACH DAY.

JESUS, PRECIOUS JESUS, HE HAS SHOWN ME THE WAY.

HALLELUJAH! PRAISE JESUS' NAME!

HE LOVES YOU AND ME, EACH AND EVERYONE THE SAME!

JESUS MY PRECIOUS JESUS I WILL FOLLOW YOU,

AND TO FORSAKE YOU I WOULD NEVER EVER DO!

JESUS HOW I LOVE YOU, I KNOW YOUR LOVE IS TRUE;

FOR WHO GAVE HIS LIFE FOR US BUT YOU!

I WILL FOLLOW THE PATH HE HAS SHOWN ME,

AND LEAD OTHERS TO IT SO THEY MIGHT SEE:

THAT HE DIED OUR SAVIOUR TO BE;

YES, HE WENT TO SLEEP THAT WE MIGHT SEE!

"Jesus Needs You to Sow Seeds"

WHO WILL CARRY SEEDS FOR THE LORD AND SOW THEM?

IF THE LORD SENDS A SEED TO YOU TO SOW,

WHAT WILL YOUR ACTION BE? WILL YOU SPEAK TO THEM?

HE SENT THE MESSAGE OUT SO THEY CAN GROW!

HIS SEEDS ARE FOR SPREADING HIS WORD TO MEN

IN NEED OF ENXCOURAAGEMENT TO KNOW "HIM."

THE SEED WAS NOT GIVEN TO OTHERS WHEN

YOU SO EASILY COULD GO TALK TO THEM!

YOU WILL RECEIVE IN TURN MANY BLESSINGS!

NO DEED GOES UNSEEN BY THE "HOLY ONE."

ALL YOU NEED DO IS DROP A LITTLE SEED,

"HE" WILL ARRANGE THE PLACE, ALSO THE TIME!

THESE SEEDS HELP KEEP HEAVENS SIRCLE OPEN!

KEEP THE FAMILY CIRCLE UNBROKEN!

"MAY THE CIRCLE BE UNBROKEN, BY AND BY LORD, BY AND BYE!

"Jesus Spoke Follow Me"

I WAS POOR, QUIET AND SHY; FAR FROM MY COUNTRY HOME.
A LITTLE CHILD WAS I, BUT JESUS SPOKE TO ME. "COME."

HE SPOKE OH COME FOLLOW ME, I'LL FORGIVE YOU CHILD YOUR SIN.
I COULD SEE THE NAIL SCARS, AND WANTED TO EVER LIVE FOR HIM.

HE SENT ME PEACE IN TIME OF NEED THROUGH A LONG AND HARD LIFE.
HE SPOKE; "I AM WITH THEE," WHEN I WAS CAUGHT IN STRIFE.

HE SET ME FREE FROM SATAN; TO LIVE LIFE PURE AND GOOD
FREE OF SIN AND HATE, AND LEADS ME TO DO AS I SHOULD.

HE PROMISES AN ABUNDANT LIFE IF WE JUST LET HIM LEAD.
HE PAID A PRICE, HIS LIFE! "JUST FOLLOW ME;" HE DOTH PLEAD."

NOW I HAVE LIFE EVER AND EVER IN HEAVEN AFTER EARTH
SATAN CAN GET ME NEVER, I'M GOD'S CHILD BY REBIRTH!

"Jesus, The Miracle Man"

HE TURNED WATER INTO WINE, CLEANSED THE TEMPLE FINE!
GAVE THE SERMON ON THE MOUNT, HE MADE DEMONS GO OUT!
HAD PARABLES TO TELL AND TAUGHT MERCY AS WELL.
"JESUS THE MIRACLE MAN"

HE MADE 5,000 DISHES FROM ONE BOYS' FISHES,
RAISED LAZ-RUS FROM THE DEAD, UP OUT OF HIS BED!
GOD SAID "HE'S MY SON," HE WALKED ON WATER SOME!
"JESUS THE MIRACLE MAN"

SAID; "ZACHEAS, COME WITH ME; DOWN OUT OF THAT TREE!"
WASHED HIS DISCIPLES FEET, SAT WITH FRIENDS TO EAT.
MADE A BLIND MAN TO SEE, SAT KIDS ON HIS KNEE!
"JESUS THE MIRACLE MAN"

"Jordan"

I GET SO EXCITED TO THINK OF JORDAN SO SWEET;

AND HOW THE WATER WILL SOOTHE MY TIRED SWOLLEN FEET.

I CAN PICTURE THE WATER, SO PRETTY, CLEAR AND BLUE:

AND PICTURE "HEAVEN" ON THE OTHER SIDE: FOR ME AND YOU.

THE STREETS ARE MADE OF GOLD, PEARLS AND JEWELS WE'LL SEE THERE!

HEAVEN GLOWS BRIGHTER AND SHINIER THAN ANYWHERE:

WE'LL SEE THE FACE OF JESUS, AND SEE OUR LOVED ONES TOO;

OUR JESUS IS PREPARING A HOME THERE FOR ME AND YOU!

OVER JORDAN: NO PARENTS WILL BREAK THEIR CHILDRENS HEARTS;

BEAT AND BRUISE THEM, TEAR THEIR WORLD APART.

THERE WILL BE NO DIVORCE, TO CAUSE CHILDREN PAIN,

AND NO NEED FOR CHILDREN RISING AGAINST PARENTS AGAIN!

O'ER THE SWEET WATERS OF JORDAN THERE WILL BE NO TEARS.

THERE WILL BE NO PAIN, NO DISEASE EVER TO FEAR.

WE WILL MEET ALL OUR LOVED ONES WAY ACROSS OVER THERE!

THINKING OF JORDAN I SEE SWEET HAPPINESS EVERYWHERE!

"Joyce"

I SAID A PRAYER FOR YOU TODAY,

AND KNOW GOD MUST HAVE HEARD.

I FELT THE ANSWER IN MY HEART,

ALTHOUGH HE SPOKE NO WORD!

I DIDN'T ASK FOR WEALTH OR FAME,

I KNEW YOU WOULDN'T MIND.

I ASKED HIM TO SEND TREASURES

OF A FAR MORE LASTING KIND.

I ASKED THAT HE'D BE NEAR YOU

AT THE START OF EACH NEW DAY,

TO GRANT YOU HEALTH AND BLESSINGS

AND FRIENDS TO SHARE YOUR WAY.

I ASKED FOR HAPPINESS FOR YOU

IN ALL THINGS GREAT AND SMALL:

BUT IT WAS FOR HIS LOVING CARE

I PRAYED FOR MOST OF ALL!

"Just One More Lord"

ONE MORE, LYING IN BED SICK AND DYING;

ONE MORE, SUICIDAL, TOO TIRED OF TRYING:

LET US BRING YOU ONE MORE LORD, JUST ONE MORE!

ONE MORE STRUGGLING WOE BEGONE YOUNG FATHER;

ONE MORE TEARFUL, DEPRESSED SINGLE MOTHER;

LET US BRING YOU ONE MORE LORD, JUST ONE MORE!

ONE MORE TEEN; FROM THIS WORLD FALLING UNDER;

PLEASE NOT YET LORD, I HEAR WARNING THUNDER!

JUST ONE MORE DROWNING SOUL LORD, JUST ONE MORE!

ONE MORE CHILD, LORD, BEATEN, BATTERED AND BLEEDING;

ONE MORE WHO LACKS LOVE AND CARE, NEEDS FEEDING!

JUST ONE MORE SWEET CHILD MY LORD; JUST ONE MORE!

ONE MORE HELPLESS WIDOW ROCKING ALONE,

ONE MORE GRAND- FATHER SITTING ALONE AT HOME,

ANOTHER LONELY SOUL LORD, YES, ONE MORE!

JUST ONE MORE LORD, CRUEL, MEAN, HARDENED SINNER;

LORD MAKE THEM ALL FISHERS OF MEN, NOT DINNER.

YES LORD, ONE MORE SOUL FOR YOU LORD, FOR YOU!

"Just Wait Kids"

WHEN I WAS YOUNG I MINDED MY MAMA,

AND I ALWAYS DID WHAT PAPA SAID,

UP UNTIL THE DAY I MARRIED,

UNTIL THE DAY I WAS WED.

NOW I MIND MY HUSBAND,

AND I TEND TO ALL HIS NEEDS.

YET MY CHILDREN WON'T BEHAVE AT ALL,

THEY'RE SOUR AS PERSIMMON SEEDS!

SO WHEN I GET OLD AND GRAY HEADED,

AND THEIR CHILDREN WON'T MIND THEM:

I'M GONNA' LAY BACK IN THAT OL' ROCKER,

AND CHUCKLE LIKE AN OL' FAT LAYIN' HEN.

"Keep Heavens' Circle Open"

MAN OF OUR FAMILY AND FRIENDS ARE LOST TODAY!
THEY WLL MISS OU ON HEAVEN; NOT KNOIW HE WAY!
WILL YOU CRY FOR THEM YOU DID NOT THE GREAT GOSPEL SHARE?
WILL THEY WONDER AND ASK IF YOU DID NOT CARE?

PLEASE GO TELL THEM NOW BEFORE IT BECOMEWWS TOO LATE
FOR THEM TO PASS ON THROUGH HEAVENS GOLDEN GATES
JUDGEMENT DAY WILL YOU SEE THEM THROWN INTO THE FIRE
WILL YOU CRY IF THEY ASK IF YOU DID NOT CARE?

HEAVENS' CIRCLE WILL GROW WITH EACH ONE WHO SEES
THE LIGHT; AND IN OUR PRECIOUS JESUS BELIEVES
JESUS TOL PETER; "FEED MY SHEEP." BEFORE HE AROSE
KEEP HEAVENS' CIRCLE OPEN BEFORE IT IS CLOSED!

"Kelly Bryant"

SWEET BEAUTIFUL BABY YOU LOOK SO TINY, SO CUTE!
YOU HAD TO GET THAT SHOCK OF BLACK HAIR FROM DADDY
AND HAD TO GET THAT SOFTNESS FROM YOUR MOTHER TO BOOT.
YOU ARE A PRECIOUS MIRACLE EVERY WHICH WAY!

WISH YOU COULD TALK TO ME LITTLE KELLY DEAR
WHAT YOU THINK WHEN YOU SMILE SO VERY SWEET
WOULD CERTAINLY BE VERY INTERESTING TO HEAR!
THOSE FACES YOU MAKE; WHAT ARE YOUR DREAMS?

MY, I WISH YOU COULD STAY LONGER TINY LITTLE DOLL.
I COULD LEARN MORE ABOUT YOU PLAY WITH YOU AWHILE.
"TIS A WONDER BEING SO PRETTY IS NOT AGAINST THE LAW.
I KNOW YOU WOULD BE ARRESTED FOR THAT SWEET SMILE!

Kimberly"

THOSE BLACK RINGLETS, OH HOW THEY CURL!
TWAS NEVER A PRETTIER SWEETER LITTLE GIRL.

A LITTLE AWEETHEART TRUE; BABY HANDS AND FACE;
THEN AS CHILDREN GROW, YOU GREW WITH GRACE.

YOU'VE EMBARKED UPON THE TIME OF WOMAN-HOOD,
GROWN SWEETER AND PRETTIER AS I KEWW YOU WOULD!

BUT ALWAYS DEAR, TO ME YOU ARE A PART,
I LOVE YOU HONEY FROM THE BOTTOM OF MY HEART!

STILL, AS ALWAYS; EMBEDDED WITHIN MY HEART
IS THE CHILD, THE WOMAN; NEAR OR FAR APART! I LOVE YOU!

"Lee Ann"

SOMEDAY OVER JORDAN WILLTRAVEL YOUR TIRED FEET;

SOON TO WALK STREETS OF GOLD AND SWEET JESUSMEET!

YOU WILL HAVE NO MORE SORROW, NOR CRY ANYMORE;

JESUS WILL DRY YOUR TEARS, YOU'LL HAVE COMFORT EVER MORE!

ALL YOUR WORK AND KINDNEWW HE SEES WITH KNOWING EYES.

WITHIN HIS ARMS OF COMFORT YOU WILL SAY NO MORE GOOD-BYES!

"Life is Equal"

FROM SHACK OR MANSION, IN SACK CLOTH OR IN SATIN
SPEAKING FLUENTLY; COMMON DIALECT OR PURE LATIN

WITH MORALS HIGH OR LOW; APPEARANCE DIRTY, CLEAN
ATHIEST BELIEF, OR GODLY; DISPOSITION GOOD OR MEAN

DEMOCRATIC OR COMMUNIST, BLACK, RED, DARK, LIGHT
IF PHYSICALLY WEAK OR STRONG; BRAVE OR AFRAID TO FIGHT

HOLDING TO ONES' BELIEFS, HIDING THOUGHTS OF THE MIND
EDUCATED OR IGNORANT, DEAF, MUTE, CRIPPLED OR BLIND

BETWIXT OR BETWEEN, UNSURE, PAST, PRESENT. UNSEEN
"EACH LIFE"
COMES INTO THE WORLD BRAND NEW, DECISIONS TO CALL
HOPES LARGE OR SMALL, RICH OR POOR, TO EACH AND TO ALL

"Line 'em Up, Bring 'em on In"

LINE 'EM UP AND BRING 'EM ON IN HERE!

THOSE BEAUTIFUL SOULS DROWNING IN SIN!

THEY ARE IN REAL NEED, LOST OUT THERE;

AND CAN'T FIND A LINE TO GET TOWED IN!

LINE THAT GOOD OL' SINNER UP AND THEN:

GOD THROUGH YOU WILL GIVE HOPE AGAIN!

SOON THINGS WILL REALLY START TO MOVE!

THROW LOVE OUT THERE; IT IS GODS' BAIT.

THE DROWNING SOUL "OUR GOD WILL SOOTHE,

THEN SAVE WITH HIS SWEET BLEESSED GRACE!

WHEN GOD CAUSES THAT OL' SINNER TO BITE,

YANK THAT LINE!" "DON'T WAIT OR HESITATE!

PULL WITH ALL YOUR LOVE; ALL YOUR MIGHT,

TOW THAT SWEET SOUL OUT BEFORE TOO LATE!"

LINE 'EM ON UP AND BRING 'EM ALL ON IN,

E'RE THEY DROWN IN PAIN AND HEART-ACHE!

"GIVE 'EM A LOVE LINE, A WAY OUT OF SIN!

PULL THEM OUT OF DRINK, DOPE, PAIN AND HATE!

"Listen and Watch"

"LISTEN,"

TO THE WHISPERING OF THE OLD OAK TREE

TO THE SONG OF A MOCKING BIRD.

DO YOU HEAR THE BUZZING OF A BEE?

"LISTEN,"

DO YOU HEAR A BABY'S CRY?

OR WAS IT THE BABBLING OF A BROOK?

THE WEEDS SHOOK, I WONDER WHY.

"WATCH,"

THE BREEZE BLEW SOFTLY THROUGH THE GRASS,

THE FLIGHT OF A SOARING HAWK.

WATCH THE FOREST ANIMALS AS THEY PASS.

"WATCH,"

WATCH THE OWL AS HE PASSES IN THE NIGHT.

WAS THAT A SPARROW FLITTING BY?

BEAUTIFULLY, GOD MAKES THINGS JUST RIGHT!

"Little Blossom"

YOUNG MAIDEN, SO BEAUTIFUL, SO YOUNG AND SO FAIR;

SEEMS YESTERDAY A CHILD, NOW MATURE, A BEAUTY RARE!

STILL INNOCENT AND SWEEET; WITH ADULT YEARNINGS: TORN;

HOW WILL YOU REPLY TO NATURES' CALLINGS; SO NEW-BORN?

BURDENED FOR THE MAID I PRAYED, "LORD HELP ME PORTRAY

THE IMPORTANCE TO HER, OF PURITY IN THIS DAY."

GOD'S PROMISE CAME TO MY MIND; "SEEK AND YE SHALL FIND"

THEN I CRIED; "LORD PLEASE HELP MY WORDS TO REACH HER MIND!"

SUDDENLY, THE ANSWER WAS SHOWN PLAINLY TO ME!

SEEING ANIMALS, I KNEW: MAN IS MADE DIFFERENTLY!

LOWLY WILD ANIMLS, HAVE NOT MANS' SOUL, MANS' MIND:

ONLY BASE INSTINCTS; TO A SOUL MATE, TO MORALS: BLIND!

GOD SHAPED MAN IN HIS OWN IMAGE, WITH STANDARDS HIGH.

GOD GAVE PRECIOUS LIFE, YOUR BODY IS A HOLY PRIZE!

SWEET MAIDEN YOU ARE SO PRECIOUS TO GOD ABOVE!

YOU'RE LIKE A BUDDING ROSE, AND AS PURE AS A WHITE DOVE!

WAIT FOR A MATE, HEAVEN PLANNED; IN HONOR AND PRIDE!

STAY A VIRGIN BLOSSOM, 'TILL GOD PUTS HIM AT YOUR SIDE!

"Little Teen"

YOU MAY THINK YOU HAVE PROBLEMS NOW MY LITTLE TEEN;

BUT INNOCENT PRINCESS DO NOT RUSH TOO SOO TO BE QUEEN!

ONE DAY ALL TOO SOON YOU WILL BE DOING AS I AM DOING NOW,

YOU'LL HEAR AN OLD FAVORITE ON RADIO AND WONDER HOW

NEARLY TEN YEARS HAVE SLIPPED BY SINCE THAT ONE CAME OUT:

AND NOW SO MUCH TIME HAS PASSED SINCE I STARTED GOING OUT.

WALK THROUGH YOUR TEENS SLOWLY, GROWN- UP INNOCENT BABE.

THEY ARE THE MOST PRECIOUS YEARS OF LIFE GOD HAS GAVE.

BE CAREFUL WITH THAT SAD LITTLE ACHE FOR SOME MAN TO CARE,

FOR IT CAN EASILY MISLEAD YOU; A WRONG PARTNER YOU MAY SHARE!

A TEEN YEARNS AND ACHES TO BE LOVED, TO BE HELD AND CARED FOR,

BUT DO NOT LET HIS CARE BLIND YOU, YOU HAVE TO KNOW FOR SURE!

IT MAY ONLY BE A FULLFILLMENT OF YOUR YEARNING FOR LOVE

YOU MAY ONLY THINK YOUR HEART HAS FOUND A TRUE LOVE!

REAL LOVE MAY STILL BE HIDDEN DEEP AND WAITING FOR ITS BEAU.

YOU MAY MISTAKE YOUR LOVE FOR THE WANT

OF SOMEONE TO HOLD YOU.

WHEN THE REAL THING COMES ALONG BE SURE YOU KNOW.

THEN AND ONLY THEN WILL YOU BE HAPPY, WILL YOUR HEART GLOW!

"Lone, Lost Child"

HE LOOKED AT HIS MAMA, HE LOOKED AT HIS DAD

HE LOOKED AT YOU. HE LOOKED AT ME

HE DIDN'T WANT TO BE; HIS SOUL COULD SEE!

(HE ASKED ME TO WRITE A POEM FROM THE LINES ABOVE.)

HE LOOKED AT HIS MAMA, AT HIS DAD; AT THE WORLDS EVIL IT BRED.

HE LOOKED AT ME, YOU; HE DIDN'T WANT TO BE, LIFE WAS CRUEL!

HIS FACE, FORLORN; HIS SOUL, SAD; FOR THE

EVIL WORLD; THE PEOPLE BAD?

HE HURT TO SEE PAIN; HE WAS MADE TO KILL ANIMALS BY HIS DAD!

A FATHER HARSH; SWEET MOTHER CALMING

HIM; HE WAS CAUGHT IN BETWEEN!

I LOVED THE LAD WITH A HEART SO SWEET,

LATER LOVED THE CONFUSED TEEN.

CONFUSED AND EMOTIONAL; MIS-UNDERSTOOD:

SOME LAUGHED; CALLED HIM MAD!

FILLED WITH CONFUSION; WEIGHTED DOWN

WITH WOE, HE DRANK; ANGER RULED!

I LOVED HIM, TRIED TO PROTECT HIM; BUT LITTLE COULD A SISTER DO!

OLDER NOW, HE'S HAUNTED BY HIS PAST. LORD

GIVE HIM PEACE FOR THIS WHILE!

PROTECT HIM FROM INFLUENCE OF OTHERS

AND FROM HIS NIGHT MARES NOW!

(THIS POEM TOOK LONGER; WAS HARDER TO WRITE

THAN ANY THING ELSE I'VE WRITTEN!

"Lord Bless My Kitchen"

LORD BLLESS MY KITCHEN AND OPEN WIDE
ITS' WELCOME TO OTHERS WHEN THEY COME.
AND THOUGH MY COOKING MAY BE JUST FINE;
IT'S NOT UP TO THE COLONELS' KENTUCKY FRIED!

HUMBLE THE MAN WHO BRINGS HOME THE CHECKS
AND HELP ME TO GET ACROSS
THAT MY FACILLITIES ARE NOT COMPLETELY AT LOSS;
AND I'M STILL DUE SOME RESPECTS!

THOUGH I TRY IT SEEMS SO HARD TO COOK
WHEN CHORES ARE RUNNING END TO END;
AND ALWAYS JUST AS SOMETHING I MEED TO BLEND;
THE RECEIPES TORN OUT OF THE AGED BOOK!

THE CHILDREN INTERRUPT, SOON I'M SPENT:
MUST CATASTROPHIES ALL COME AT SUPPERTIME?
SEEMS THE KNACK OF COOKING JUST ISN'T MINE.
YOU KNOW LORD I NEED YOUR HELP: HEAVEN SENT!

"Lord Give Me Wisdom"

LORD GIVE ME WISDOM TO SEE THE GOOD IN OTHERTS THOU DOST SEE;

TO LOOK THRU THE FLAWS AND SEE THE GOOD HIDDEN FROM ME.

WHEN MY BROTHER DOES A WRONG AND IT HURTS DEEP

REMIND ME DEAR LORD THAT PERFECT WE CAN'T ALWAYS KEEP!

MY SIGHT IS NOT PERFECT AND IN SAYING "HE'S WRONG," I JUDGE:

HUMBLE ME THAT I JUDGE NOT AND WITH
MY BROTHER, HOLD NO GRUDGE.

FORGIVE THEM LORD, THE ONES IN WRONG;
THEY KNOW NOT WHAT THEY DO.

LET ME GIVE MY BROTHER ALWAYS A HELPING
HAND: LEAVE THE REST TO YOU!

"Lord I Need Thee"

"THANKSGIVING AND CHRISTMAS HOLIDAYS ARE NEAR
WITH FOOD AND GIFTS, THANKFULNESS AND CHEER.
I'M SATISFIED THOUGH MY CUPBORD DOES NOT HOLD THE BEST.
I CAN OVER-LOOK THAT LORD, I T'S JUST THE REST.

MY BROTHER IS OUT OF WORK, HAD TO SEND HIS WIFE AND BABE AWAY.
GRANDMA AND GRANDPA ARE SICK, LONELY AND ALONE.
DAD HAS NO ONE BUT ME AND MY FAMILY TO MAKE HIM GAY.
MY SISTER HAS BEEN DESERTED BECAUSE MOM HAS GONE.
MOM JUST UP AND WENT AWAY WITHOUT A WORD TO ANYONE.
SHE CAN STAY WITH ME, BUT THEY'ERE ALL
IN NEED OF HELP AND CHEER.
I DON'T KNOW WHAT TO DO OR WHO TO HELP, I CAN HELP SOME,
BUT NOT ALL, SOMEONE WILL BE LEFT OUT I FEAR.

THEN I HAVE MY KIDS AND HUSBAND AND BABE ON THE WAY.
WHAT WILL THEY ALL DO? LORD, ALL I CAN DO IS PRAY.
I HAVE MY OWN TO CHEER AND CANNOT HELP THEM ALL.
WHICH WAY LORD, CAN I BE TH EMOST HELP OF ALL?

"Lord I Thank You"

"LORD IT SEEMS YOU KEEP TENDING TO MY NEEEDS:
IT'S MIRACULOUS YOU KNOW! I SO WANTED A
CHOCOLATE CAKE AND HAD NO CHOCOLATE. IN THE
MIDST OF MY CRAVINGS, A NEIGHBOR BROUGHT
ME ONE! I'VE NOT BEEN MOVED IN LONG, LORD. YOU
MUST HAVE SENT HER WORD THAT I LOVE
CHOCOLATE! SUCH A SMALL THING LORD, AND YOU
CARED, IT BRINGS TEARS TO MY EYES LORD.
WHO AM I THAT YOU SHOULD TEND THESE LITTLE
MATTERS? I THANK YOU OH LORD!
I HAVE MOST OF MY HOUSE IN ORDER NOW BUT ALL
MY PICTRES ARE'NT HUNG. I WAS AT A LOSS
AS WHAT TO HANG ON AN EMPTY WALL IN THE KITCHEN:
LO, ANOTHER NEIGHBOR PAINTED ME A
BEAUTIFUL PICTURE OF THE POMEGRANITE. IT WEILL
GO SO WELL THERE: SIZE, COLOR AND WHAT I
LIKE!
THEN TODAY: FRIDAYS GET A LUITTLE LONELY AND
I'M USUALLY IMPATIENT. SUPPER IS RATHER
DULL BECAUSE THE CUPBOARD IS NO LONGER FULL. I
LOOKED OUT THE WINDOW AND SAW TO MY
SURPRISE, COMPANY FOR ME, ON A RESTLESS DAY! HOW
GENEROUS OF YOU LORD! IT WAS PEGGY; A
COUSIN I HADN'T SEEN IN YEARS: AND WHAT DID SHE
DO BUT BRING SAUSAGE FROM HER OWN PIG

AND GREEN BEANS FROM HER SUMMER GARDEN. THAT

WLL, ADD QUIET A SAVOR TO MY OTHERWISE

DULL SUPPER TONIGHT! AGAIN THANK YOU LORD! PEGGY

TOOK ME TO GRANDADS GRAVE; THE FIRST

TIME I'VE GO TO GO. HER FATHEER LIES NEAR THERE

NOW: HOW MUCH CLOSER THIS HAS MADE US

TODAY! BLESS HER LORD FOR HER DUTIFUL DAY;

MAY YOURS BE THE GLORY I EVER PRAY!

P.S. LORD, PLEASE HELP ME TO REPAY THESE DEBTS.

"Lord Lead Me on Thy Path"

LORD, I'M ANXIOUS TO TRAVEL, LEAD ON. THOUGH
THE JOURNEY IS ROUGH I'LL GO,
SO LEAD ME NOW LORD, LEAD ME ON; TO
WHERE THY CRYSTAL WATERS FLOW!

WHEN I GET THERE I'LL BE WEARY; THERE I'LL
COOL MY DUST-TRODDEN FEET,
RINSE AWAY CARE FOR MY JOURNEY; THERE
OTHER TRAVELERS I WILL MEET!

THE PATH MAY BE DUSTY AND DRY 'NEATH THE SCORCHING SUN
WE'LL REACH COOL WATER BYE AND BYE: SOAK
IN CONTENTMENT, VICTORY WON!

I KNOW LORD THE WAY'S HARD AND STEEP. I'LL
FOLLOW ON THRU THAT LAST MILE
NOT TARRY 'LONG THE WAY, BUT KEEP FAST
ON THE NARROW PATH AND SMILE!

PERHAPS I'LL MEET ALONG THE WAY OTHERS
WHO FOLLOW 'LONG THE PATH.
WE'LL RINSE OFF THE DUST AND CLAY IN THY
COOL SOOTHING CRYSTAL BATH!

HELP ME LORD WHEN I MEET A FRIEND SHOW

JUST HOW THEY CAN ALSO GO!

TELL HOW YOU DIED FOR ALL THEIR SINS HOW

YOU TURNED THEM WHITE AS SNOW!

WHEN I REACH THE WATERS COOL AND CLEAR;

SIT, REST; PARTAKE OF HOLY BREAD;

MAY I SOON BE JOINED BY OTHERS DEAR WHO'VE

FOLLOWED THY WAY AND THY GOSPEL SPREAD?

"Lord Thank You for My Girls"

THANK YOU LORD FOR MY THREE LITTLE GIRLS.

THE OLDEST IS A LITTLE LADY, SO BIG, SO SMALL!

THE SECOND IS JUST A SWEET LITTLE DARLING WITH CURLS:

AND THE NEW BABY LORD IS PRECIOUS, SO NEW AND ALL!

GRANT ME TIME TO GIVE EACH A MOTHERS' LOVE AND CARE.

GIVE ME PATIERNCE, UNDERSTANDING, AND A LOVING HEART.

FOR MY HUSBAND, TEACH ME TO GIVE AND TO ALWAYS SHARE

AND MAY I KEEP A WARM HEART, A TENDER SMILE, LEST WE PART.

IT SEEMS LORD THAT PERRHAPS I'VE ASKED TOO MUCH;

BUT I HAVE ANOTHER REQUEST DEAR LORD, JUST ONE.

SOMEDAY MAY I HAVE: TO HOLD, TO SEE, TO LOVE, TO TOUCH:

IN ADDITION TO THE GIRLS, LORD PLEASE GRANT ME A SON.

"Lord You've Always Been There"

I'VE WRITTEN PRAYERS ASKING YOUR FORGIVENESS

AND I'VE WRITTEN SEVERAL PRAYERS OF JOY!

I'VE WRITTEN PRAYERS ASKING FOR ANSWERS:

I'VEWRITTEN A PRAYER PLEADING FOR A BABY BOY!

I'VE WRITTEN PRAYERS ASKING HELP FOR OTHERS;

PRAYERS FOR STRENGTH FOR WHAT MOTHERS MUST BE.

I'VE WRITTEN PRAYERS FOR THE HEALTH OF MY CHILDREN

AND I'VE WRITTEN THANKS FOR WHAT YOU'VE GIVEN ME!

I REMEMBER THE DAY LORD THAT YOU SAVED MY SOUL:

AND 'OFT FOR ONE PERSON I'VE BEEN BLESSED, YOU'VE BEEN REAL!

WHEN JUST FIFTEEN I SAW WITH EYES OF MINE OWN

THINE HOLY HAND: WITH ME IN A STRANGE LAND, EVEN STILL!

IT WAS A GENTLE REMINDER TO MY SADDENED HEART

THAT WHERE E'ER I GO YOU'RE WITH ME EVER

AND NEVER MUST I FACE LIFES CHALLENGES ALONE.

I HAVE HAD YOUR PROTRECTION WITH ME WHEREEVER!

THROUGH ALL MY LIFES' STRUGGLES YOU GAVE ME STRENGTH.

YOU GAVE MEJOY IN THER LIFE THAT I CHOSE!

ALWAYS WHEN I NEEDED YOU, YOU WERE EVER THERE

AND GAVE ABILITY TO ME THAT ABOVE SADDNESS I ROSE!

"Love"

LOVE IS LIKE THE SUNSHINE THAT MAKES THE ROSES GROW;
FOR LOVE BLOOMS FORTH GOODNESS IN OTHERS THAT WE KNOW.

TOO SEVERE HOT SUNSHINE CHOKES AND KILLS PLANT LIFE;
AS LOVING ONE FIERCELY BREEDSS JELOUSLY, CAUSES STRIFE.

TOO MILD AND DISTANT SUNSHINE CAUSES GROWTH TO WANE;
AS LUKE WARM LOVE FOR ANOTHER WILL NOT LAST, BUT SLOWLY FADE.

A WARM LASTING SUNSHINE WITH MILD WIND DOES REAP BEST;
AS DEEP LOVE WITH UNDERSTANDING CAUSES LOVE TO EVER LAST!

GOD IS MANS' SUNSHINE THAT MAKES THE HEART GLOW
HE BLOOMS IN US GOODNESS SO THAT HIS LOVE SHOWS.

HE IS A DEEP LASTING SUNSHINE, THE HOLY SPIRIT WIND WE NEED;
TO BLOOM FORTH SMILING FLOWERS FROM HUMAN EARTHLY SEED!

"Loves Happiness Gate"

I'VE LIVED A FULL LIFE AS FAR AS LIVING GOES

THE JOYS I'VE SEEN ONLY GOD ABOVE KNOWS.

I'VE KNOWN LOVE AS ONLY TRUE LOVE KNOWS.

I'VE SEEN THAT KNOWING AND SHARING MAKE LOVE GROW!

LOVING ONE SO MUCH, THAT ONE YOU CAN NEVER HATE;

EVEN WHEN HE'S GONE YOU KNOW, TIS ONLY YOUR FATE!

BUT LOVE COMES ONLY ONCE, THEN IT'S TOO LATE.

ONCE HE'S GONE YOU'RE LEFT OUTSIDE "LOVES' HAPPINESS GATE!"

YOU LOVED HIM WELL DEAR HEART; BUT THE GATE IS SHUT TIGHT!

WORK, HELP OTHERS; WHEN LONELY PRAY MORE THAT NIGHT!

AS LONG AS YOU'RE WORKING, PRAYING, GIVING; YOU WILL BE ALRIGHT!

COUNT EVERY BLESSINGS WHEN YOU LAY AWAKE LATE AT NIGHT!

LOVE'S HAPPINESS GATE IS CLOSED, BUT HEAVENS' OPEN WIDE.

THE GATE OF HEAVEN IS OPEN, JESUS IS ALWAYS BY YOUR SIDE!

WORK, REACH YOUR GOALS AND ALWAYSS KEEP YOUR PRIDE.

NEVER ABOVE ALL FORGET TO PRAY: HEAVEN'S ON YOUR SIDE!

"Mamma"

"MAMA, I'M FEELING MUCH BETTER!"

"HEY, GUESS WHO I TALKED TO TODAY."

'I'M WRITING YOU THIS LETTER;

I'D CALL; BUT HEAVEN'S TOO FAR AWAY!"

"I HEARD A NEW SONG ON RADIO,

THE KIND BOTH OF US LIKE SO WELL."

"I KNOW YOU WOULD HAVE LIKED IT TOO;

I PICKED UP THE PHONE, MY HEART FELL."

"MAMMA, ONLY YOU UNDERSTOOD

THE LITTLE SPECIAL WAYS WE SHARED."

"OH THE HEARTBREAKS SO TENDERLY SOOTHED

BY YOUR VOICE ON THE PHONE: YOU CARED!"

SO MANY THINGS YOU'VE SAID AND DONE;

TO MAKE ME FEEL PROUD; NOT TO FALL!"

"THE ACHE, THE CHEER, THE BATTLE WON:

OH, MAMMA; IT HURTS WHEN I CAN'T CALL!"

"TIME EASES GRIEFS BITTER-SWEET PAIN

YOU HAVE OFTEN SAID: WAS WELL KNOWN."

"YET, MAMMA; TIMER AND TIME AGAIN,

PAIN COMES BACK WHEN I PICK UPTHE PHONE!"

"Marie"

CHILDHOOD IS THE REAL TIME
WHEN WE'RE FREE FOR WHAT WE FEEL TIME
THEN MOLDING OF OUR GOALS TIME
THE SWEET PRECIOUS LAUGHTER PEEL TIME!

GROWING UP IS TRIAL AND ERROR TIME
OFTEN OUR BACK UP AND PUNT OVER TIME
ROCKING THE BABY AND SIGHING TIME
BUT DON'T LET IT BE DREAM DYING TIME!

HOLD TIGHT TO THE LITTLE CHILD INSIDE
HOLD ON TO THE HOPE AND PRIDE
THE CHILD OF TRUTH WITH DREAMS ABIDE
LET HER EVER THRU LIFE WALK BY YOUR SIDE!

"Marsha"

LEARN PATIENCE MY FRIEND WHILE YET YOU ARE YOUNG,
FOR IT IS A TRYING WORLD THAT WE MUST LIVE AMONG

DRAW STRENGTH FROM ABOVE WHEN LIFE TROUBLES YOU:
JEESUS' SMILING FACE EVER SEES WHEN YOU ARE BLUE.

IT'S HARD TO ENDURE CRITICISM, ESPECIALLY FOR SOME,
REMEMBER, WITH AGE THEY'LL REMEMBER
THE WRONG THEY HAVE DONE.

BRACE YOURSELF, CARRY ON, KEEP AN OPEN EYE FOR FAULTS,
USUSALLY THERE'S SOME CAUSE FOR THOSE CRITICAL THOUGHTS.

GOD ALWAYS SHOWS THE WAY IF WE'RE WILLING TO SEE,
AND EVERYTHING ENDS UP BEAUTIFUL, AS GOD PLANNED IT TO BE!

"Misty"

I LOVE YOU MISTY, MY DARLING, DARLING CHILD.

YOU'RE LIKE A RARE ORCHID IN THE FOREST WILD.

HIDDEN AND LOVELY, A BEAUTY ONE SELDOM SEES,

DELICATE, YET STRONG, A SPIRIT SWEET AND FREE.

CONCEIVED IN A MOMENT, SHAPED BY GOD ABOVE.

I PRAISE HIM FOR TRHE PLEASURE TO HAVE YOU TO LOVE!

I THANK HIM FOR THE GIFT TO KNOW YOU AS I DO

AND FOR THE HELP HE'S GIVEN ME IN RAISING YOU!

YES, YOU ARE TRULY PRECIOUS MISTY, TO MY HEART;

MOLDED PERFECTLY, MY WORK ONLY A LITTLE PART.

YOUI WERE BORN WITH A SENSE OF FAIRNESS TO MAN,

A LOVE OF LAUGHTER, THE ABILTY TO UNDERSTAND.

A SWEET SHYNES LIES BEHIND THY BLUSHING CHEEK

A LAUGHTER FLOWS FROM YOU LIKE A BUBBLING CREEK;

YOU MAKE THOSE ABOUT YOU HAPPY AND CALM;

AND CARRY WITH YOUR PRESENCE A LIGHT LILTING SONG!

I WISH FOR YOU EVERY HAPPINESS YOU CAN KNOW,

AND HOPE YOU FEEL MY LOVE; OFTEN HARD TO SHOW.

YOU'RE A WIFE NOW DAUGHTER, SOON MOTHER TO BE,

BUT MY PRECIOUS DARLING MISTY YOU'LL EVER BE TO ME!

"Mom"

REMEMBER WHEN THE LITTLE BABE PICKED DANDELIONS JUST FOR YOU?

THEY WEREN'T VERY PRETTY, THEY DIDN'T

AMOUNT TO MUCH, BUT SAID;

"MOM, I LOVE YOU."

WELL, WE COULDN'T GET YOU THAT ORCHID, NOT EVEN BUY A CARD

AND SOMETIMES WHEN YOU WANT TO SPILL OUT YOUR HEART

IT'S VERY HARD!

SO THIS MAY NOT BE VERY PRETTY, WE NOW IT'S NOT A LOT,

BUT WE WANT TO TELL YOU MOTHER, WHAT A WONDERFUL MOM

WE THINK WE'VE GOT!

THE PRETTIEST ORHID AND A DOZEN ROSES

ARE BOTH RESERVED FOR YOU

AND I HOPE OUR THOUGHTS AND GOOD WISHES

TO YOUR HEART PASS THROUGH;

'CAUSE MOM, WE SURE LOVE YOU!

"Morning Sunshine"

NOTHING IS MORE CHEERFUL AND GAY
AS THE SUNSHINE AT BEGINNING OF DAY.

THE BEDROOM SLOWLY BRIGHTENS, I GET UP.
SUN SPARKLES DANCE AROUND MY COFFEE CUP.

THE WHOLE KITCHEN TURNS INTO CHEER
AS THE CHILDREN APPEAR FROM NOWHERE.

ONE BY ONE TO THE SUNNY TABLE THEY COME,
BREAKING THE MONOTONY OF THE REFRIGERATOR HUM.

THE SUN PLAYFULLY SPARKLESS ON THEIR HAIR,
THEY SEEM AS LITTLE ANGELS BRIGHT AND FAIR!

BABY TRIES TO CATCH PARTICLES IN THE SUNSHINE:
I HAVE GODS' BEAUTY AND WARMTH, HERE; ALL MINE!

"Mother, I Remember"

IT IS ALWAYS SUCH A GREAT PLEASURE TO RECALL

THE GOOD TIMES BACK WHEN I WAS VERY SMALL.

THE TINY NEW DOLL; WHY IT SOMEHOW MADE YOU FEEL

AS NEEDED AND PRECIOUS AS YOU; "FOR REAL."

ALL THE BIRTHDAYS, CHRISTMASSES; THE JOY, THE TEARS;

HAVE ALL PASSED TOO QUICKLY THROUGHOUT THE YEARS.

BEST OF ALL IS THE MEMORY OF YOUR SMILE;

THE HUGS, AND SITTING IN YOUR LAP AWHILE!

FOR THESE CHERISSHED MERMORIES I THANK GOD ABOVE;

THE GREATEST GIFT FROM MOTHER IS HER LOVE!

NO MATTER HOW GROWN-UP, HOW FAR WE'RE APART;

I'M STILL "YOUR LITTLE GIRL," DOWN IN MY HEART!

AND OFT' AS I GO THROUGH LIFES' DRAMA,

MY HEART CRIES OUT, "I STILL NEED YOU MAMMA!"

THEN FOR A MOMENT I'LL STOP AND JUST PRETEND

THAT I REAH UP ONCE MORE TO TAKE YOUR HAND!

LIKE LONG AGO, I'M YOUR LITTLE GIRL ONCE MORE;

AND WE STROLL DOWN THE LANE, JUST LIKE BEFORE,

WITH THE SUN SHINNNG BRIGHT AND LIFE ERY GAY;

SKIPPING NOW AND THEN, FULL OF LIFE AND PLAY!

MY GIRLS IN BED, ME HERE IN MY PAJAMAS!

YES, STILL YOUR LITTLE GIRL NEEDS YOU MAMMA!

"Mother is Really Leaving"

"OUR MOTHER'S LEAVING US FOR HEAVEN THIS SPRING!"

"WHEN THE SWEET VIOLETS BLOOM AND THE BIRDS SOFTLY SING."

THANK GOD FOR ALL THE SWEET MOTHERS

WHO TEACH WEE CHILDREN GODS' SWEET WONDERS!

HOW TO MAKE CHAINS FROM SIMPLE CLOVER......

SEE IMAGES IN CLOUDS THAT HOVER!

PACK PIC-NICS TO MAKE A HOLIDAY

TEACH TINY HANDS TO FOLD AND PRAY!

REMIND US OF SWEATERS IN THE FALL

POINT OUT GOLDEN LEAVES ON TREES SO TALL.

PREPARE FOR THEIR NEEDS AS THEY FROLIC

CURE TINY ILLS, WITH LOVE AS TONIC!

MAKE THE HOME WARM FROM WINTERS' COLD

PASS ON THE GOOD TRADITIONS OF OLD.

MAKE EACH YEARS NEW HOLIDAYS SO REAL'

PRECIOUS MEMORIES WE EVER FEEL!

WHO PLANT FLOWERS SO PRETTY IN SPRING

SHOW THE CHILD A JAY BIRD TAKING WING.

TEACHING BEAUTY AND JOY OF LIVING

WITH SWEET, CONSTANT, LOVE AND GIVING!

"Mount Olivet Baptist Church"

(THERE IS A HEARTBEAT INSIDE MOUNT OLIVET CHURCH.)

MOUNT OLIVET'S JUST ONE OF MANY CHURCHES IN THE WORLD.
CHURCHES ARE REFERRED TO AS "HIS BRIDE!"
CORRECT IS THE PASTOR WITH HIS SERMONS UN-FURLED
WARNING US TO BE A CHASTE PEOPLE SET ASIDE!

FOR THERE IS A HEART AND A BODY WITHIN THE CHURCH
FOR LOVE AND JOY HE AWAITS; HE LONGS!
HE BUILDS HER A HOME, WATCHING HER; HERE ON EARTH;
HOPING HER HEART BEATS FOR HIM A SOULFUL SONG!

WE ALL SING FOR HIM WHEN WE MEET TOGETHER IN CHURCH.
CHILDREN ON CHURCH BUSSES WE BRING IN:
TO TELL THEM GOD'S LOVED THEM SINCE THEIR VERY BIRTH
AND WANTS THEM TO JOIN HIM SOMEDAY IN HEAVEN!

TOGETHER WITH ONE HEARTBEAT, OUR JESUS WE AWAIT.
WE LONG TO SEE OUR HEAVENLY HOMES;
EVER LONG TO LOOK UPON HIS BLESSES FACE!
WAIT TO SING HIM PERAISES FOREVER IIN SONG!

"Moving On"

WITHIN I'M CHANGING, MOODS RE-ARRANGING.

MUST BE I'M GROWING, IS IT REALLY SHOWING?

I CAN TELL MY TASTE IN THINGS IS CHANGING;

I LIE AWAKE AND WONDER, WHERE AM I GOING?

I'VE BECOME A BETTER BUSINESS PERSON BY FAR.

QUALITIES INSIDE AWAKEN, I FORGOT WERE THERE.

EVEN MY WRITING HAS CHANGED MORE ABOVE PAR.

BUT; THE ME I BARELY KNEW, IS MOVING ON TO WHERE?

EXACTLY WHO WAS I BEFORE BEGINNING TO CHANGE:

AND WHO WILL I BECOME MYSELF TO BE?

'TIS LIKE THE OCEANS' WAVES FROM WITHIN, STRANGE;

ROLLING AND MOVING INSIDE, A FORCE PULLING ME.

WITHIN ME LIES THE GIRL, RELUCTANT TO GROW UP:

BESIDE HER, THE TWIN, THE DREAMER; CALLING; "COME."

DEEPLY HIDDEN, SO LONG AGO; I SIPPED HAPPINESS' CUP.

A SHORT SIP SO SWEET ERE LOST; I WISHED TO DIE FROM!

THEN IN REALITY: TO SIP, AGAIN HAVE I…..

TOUCHING SUCH MEMORY I CRY!

LORD THANK YOU FOR THIS HAPPINESS, MINE!

"Mr. Cross"

HE'LL BE REMEMBERED BY THE CHILDREN;
HE WAS SUCH A FRIEND AND NEIGHBOR TOO.

HE'LL KEEP A PLACE IN THE HEARTS OF MANY
'ROUND ABOUT, HE GREETED AND KNEW!

THROUGH THE LIVES OF HIS CHILDREN
HE'LL LIVE THROUGH YEARS TO COME.

HIS LOVE WILL STILL SURRUND YOU ROSIE
HE'S ONLY MOVED UPWARD, HE'S NOT GONE!

WE CAN'T KEEP A LOVED ONE AT THEIR TO GO;
AND HE WOLDN'T WANT YOU TO SUFFER SO!

TAKE COMFORT AND CARE NOW FOR YOUR LIFE:
'TWOULD BE HIS MESSAGE FOR FAMILY AND WIFE.

HIS LOVE STILL COMES DOWN NOW FROM ABOVE.
LOVED ONES TAKE COMFORT IN HIS AND GODS' LO VE!

"Music in the Family"

I CAN HEAR GRANDADDY SINGIN' JUST AS PLAIN AS DAY;

"OVER THE BLUE WATER, THERE LIVED A GERMANS' DAUGHTER;'

"PRETTY FRAULINE." AND I'M SURE HE KNEW HER O'ER THE WAY!

I CAN SEE GRANNY PLAYIN' HYMNS AND SONGS.

ON THAT OLD ACCORDIAN SHE HAD SO LONG.

GRANDADDY WAS ONCE A DRINKIN' MAN,

AND I CAN HEAR GRANNY APPLY;

"HO, HO, HO; HEE, HEE, HEE!" LITTLE BROWN JUG,

R SHE GOT IN THE RHYTHM REAL GOOD)

I STILL HEAR DAD'S HARMONICA AS HE PLAYED; "THE LITTLE MOHEE;

JUST A CRYIN' IN THE CHAPEL;" THEN ALWAYS "RED WING" FOR ME!

MAMA'S "RED SAILS IN THE SUNSET" FOR DAD, AND "COWBOY JACK;

THEN; "I'M NOT IN YOUR TOWN TO STAY, I'M

HERE TO GET MY BABY BOY OUT

OF JAIL." WITH THE LAST ONE SHE HAD US CHILDREN

WIPING HOT SALTY TEARS BACK!

MY GREAT GRANDMOTHER WOULD COME VISITIN'. SHE'D SMOKE HER OL'

CORN COB PIPE AND PAT HER FEET TO "YOU

GIT A LINE AND I'LL GIT A POLE."

I REMEMBER "BARBRY ALLEN;" "MOONLIGHT

GAMBLER;" AND "MY SCARLET LOVER:"

"THE OLD RUGGED CROSS;" "SHOT GUN BOOGY;"

"PEACE IN THE VALLEY;" AND OTHERS:

DADDY WOULD SING "BUFFALO GALS" AND IF YOU

GOT THE MONEY HONEY, I GOT THE TIME!"

WHEN HE PLAYED THE HARMONICA HE
WOULD HAVE US GUESS THE SONG.

HE'D CHALLENGE US; "I'LL GIVE YOU A PENNY IF YOU GUESS THIS SONG."

MAMMA WOULD SING; "GONNA' TAKE A SENTIMENTAL
JOURNEY," BEFORE IT WAS THROUGH.

I DIDN'T KNOW WHY BACK THEN, BUT IT WOULD ALWAYS MAKE ME BLUE.

"My Friend

I LOVE YOU INNOCENT OR IN SORROW SURE,
FOR THE LOVE OF A TRUE FRIEND IS PURE.

YET, IF I CAME THUS IN MY HUMAN WAY:
CHRIST CARES MORE; JUST TAKE TIME TO SAY;

LORD, FORGIVE THIS TRESSPASS, EVEN THIIS ONE:
AND NO SOONER DEAR FRIEND IS IT SAID THAN DONE!

SO MUCH MORE THAN I; CHRIST IS YOUR FRIEND.
HE LOVES AND HE CARES AND WILL TO THE END!

II'S SAD THAT SATAN WON A BATTLE SORE,
JUST TALK TO CHRIST FRIEND, YES, BEFORE

SATAN STEPS IN TO SNATCH ANOTHER VICTORY SUCH
AND PREVENTS YOU KNOWING GOD LOVES YOU SO MUCH!

YES, I LOVE YOU, AND NO LESS FOR WHAT'S DONE:
IF I, THEN CHRIST TOO, WAITS THE NEXT VICTORY WON!

"My Girls"

BONNIE IS MY WILD LITTLE DAISY,
MY FIRST AND ONLY ONE!
SUNSHINE BRIGHT IS HER NATURE,
SMILING LIKE THE MORNING SUN.

MISTY IS MY RARE, RARE ORCHID;
A MYSTICAL, LOVELY; EXOTIC FLOWER.
CERTAINLY THE ONLY ONE IN THE WORLD:
AND NEVER STOPS LONG ANYWHERE!

STEPHANIE IS MY TOUCH-ME-NOT
SPREADING QUICK AS A VINE.
ALWAYS GROWING IN BEAUTY. LEFT ALONE
SHE'LL SEE ALL HAVE A GOOD TIME!

GLENDA MUST BE MY YELLOW ROSE,
TENDER AND SWEET BUT STRONG.
SWEET AS HER FAVORITE CHOCOLATE PIE;
UNDERSTANDING AS THE DAY IS LONG!

"My Home"

LORD I SIT AND LOOK AROUND AND WHAT I SEE

IS TOO WONDEROUS, I CAN'T HUSH THE FEELING IT GIVES ME.

PRAYERS ARE ANSWERED EVERY SINGLE LIVING DAY

BUT IT WAS TOO GOOD OF YOU TO ANSWER MINE THIS WAY.

YET LORD I APPRECIATE IT; DON' TAKE ME WRONG,

I'D BE TERRIBLY DISSAPPOINTED IF THIS WERE ALL GONE!

IT SEEMS TOO BLISSFUL, THIS HOUSE YOU FOUND ME;

IN SIGHT OF THE RIVER, SURROOUNDED BY EVERY KIND OF TREE.

THE FLORIDA WINDOW IN MY KITCHEN I SEE THE RIVER BY,

WHY IT'S SUCH A BEAUTIFUL SIGHT TO THE HUMAN EYE!

THE SLIDING GLASS DOORS GOING OUT TO THE PATIO,

LORD I WAS DREAMING OF ONE JUST NO TIME AGO.

THE FAMILY ROOM DOWNSTAIRS IS JUST A REAL DREAM,

AND THE KIDS RUNNING UP THE HILL, HOW HAPPY THEY SEEM.

SUCH A BEAUTIFUL HOME IN THE COUNTRY, CLOSE TO CHURCH;

WHY LORD, I FEEL LIKE A BIRD NESTING ON A GOLDEN PERCH!

I PRAYED FOR A HOUSE DOWN HERE SOME WHERE ABOUTS,

BUT LORD I NEVER DREAMED OF THIS PERFECT A HOUSE!

SO THANK YOU LORD, AND WATCH, LEAST I TAKE TOO MUCH PRIDE

AND FROM ALL THIS BEAUTY, PUT YOUR BUSINESS ASIDE.

THOUGH IT DOESN'T SEEM POSSIBLE, YOU SEEM SO CLOSE NOW.

LEAD AND GUIDE ME LORD TO RETURN THE FAVOR SOMEHOW!

"My Jesus"

JUDAS BETRAYED WHILE JESUS OF NAZARETH PRAYED.

WITH A KISS, MY LORDS' IDENTITY, HE OF EVIL GAVE!

THEY NAILED HIS HANDS AND THEY NAILED HIS FEET.

THEY PIERCED HIS SIDE, AND SO FEW DID WEEP!

IN PAIN HE BLED, FOR OUR SINS, MY SAVIOR DIED.

HE HAD NO SIN OF HIS OWN, NO GREED NOR PRIDE.

HE AROSE WITH SCARS IN HIS SIDE, FEET AND HANDS;

AS VICTOR OVER DEATH, AS SAVIOR OF SINFULL MAN!

"My Jesus Lived"

HE WALKED, HE TALKED, HE LAUGHED, HE CRIED!
HE ATE, HE SLEPT, HE LIVED AND DIED!
YES, MY JESUS IS REAL, THIS I KNOW, ICAN FEEL!

JESUS KNELT UPON HIS KNEES TO PRAY.
JUDAS CAME, A KISS TO HIM GAVE:
THEN THEY PUT NAILS IN HIS HANDS AND FEET;
STABBED HIS SIDE; MADE HIS LOVED ONES WEEP!
SO, IN PAIN HE BLED, AND FOR OUR SINS HE DIED!
HE HAD NO SIN OF HIS OWN, NO GREED, NOR PRIDE!
HE AROSE WITH SCARS IN HIS SIDE, FEET AND HANDS;
AS VICTOR OVER DEATH, AS SAVIOR OF SINFUL MEN!
HE ONLY PRAYED: "THY WILL FATHER, NOT MINE OWN:"
BUT THEY BEAT HIM AND ON THE CRUEL CROSS HE HUNG!
TODAY HE SITS BY HIS FATHERS' SIDE, BECKONING STILL;
CRYING; BELIEVE UPON ME! I CAME, I DIED, NOWI LIVE!

HE WALKED, HE TALKED, HE LAUGHED, HE CRIED!
HE WALKED, HE TALKED, HE LAUGHED, HE CRIED!
HE ATE, HE SLEPT, HE LIVED, AND DIED!
YES MY JESUS IS REAL, THIIS I KNOW I CAN FEEL!

"My Little Bonnie"

MY LITTLE BONNIE, SO SHY, SO SWEET,
SHE'S TOO YOUNG, ALONE THE WORLD TO MEET!
MY LITTLE DARLING, JUST A CHILD OF THREE,
SHE'S TOO YOUNG TO BE AWAY FROM ME.

WITHOUT HER MOMMY, WITH STRANGERS TOO,
AND JUST THIS MONTH SHE'LL BE PAST TWO!
HARDLY THREE AND ON A JOURNEY ALONE.
NOW I WISH I'D TOOK BABY AND GONE ALONG!

FOUR LITTLE HOURS WILL SEEM AT LEAST A WEEK
TO HER LITTLE MIND SO INNOCENT AND SWEET.
I MISS HER; THO GOOD NEIGHBORS TOOK HER TOO;
MY BABY HAS ONLY GONE TO BIBLE SCHOOL!

"My Little House"

"EITHER MY FAMILY IS TOO BIG OR MY HOUSE TOO SMALL,"
I THINK, EACH TIME I PASS THROUGH OUR TINY HALL:
THEN JUST AS I START TO FORM A COMPLAINT IN MY MIND;
I SEE SOMEWHERE, "LOVE" OF SOME SHAPE OR KIND!
ANEW I SAY; "THANK YOU LORD FOR THIS HOUSE OF LOVE."
IN EVERY CORNER THIS HOUSE IS BLESSED FROM ABOVE!

EITHER OTHER FOLKS HAVE MORE VALUABLE THINGS THAN I,
OR AT LEAST BETTER QUALITY, AND OFT I WONDER; "WHY?"
THEN JUST AS SELF-PITY STARTS TO FLOW, SO VERY NEAR
I SEE SOME OBJECT THAT SUDDENLY BRINGS A TEAR.
ANEW, I SAY; "THANK YOU LORD FOR RICHES 'NIGH HEAVEN!"
MOST OF WHAT I HAVE, HAS OUT OF OTHERS LOVE BEEN GIVEN."

SO I THANK YOU LORD FOR MY EARTHLY HIME.
AND I THANK YOU GRACIOUSLY FOR ALL THAT'S IN IT!
BUT MOST OF ALL I THANK YOU THAT I'VE KNOWN
THESE BEAUTIFUL ONES I SHARE IT WITH; FAMILY WHO BEGIN IT!"

"My Lost World"

WHEN I WAS A TEENAGE GIRL,
NEAR THE BEACH IN MY OWN WORLD:
AT NIGHT MY THOUGHTS TRAVELED DEEP;
BUT THE OCEAN SOUNDS ROCKED ME TO SLEEP.

I'M A WIFE AND MOTHER NOW.
I'VE LOST MY OWN LITTLE WORLD SOMEHOW.
WORK, ERRANDS, APOINTMENTS TO KEEP:
THE FAMILY TO GET SETTLED DOWN TO SLEEP.

WHISPERING SOUNDS OF OCEAN WAVES,
THOUGHTS, DREAMS, FROM THOSE GOLDEN DAYS;
MY WORLD IS LOST DEEP IN TIME SOMEHOW
AND I NEED TO BE ROCKED GENTLY TO SLEEP NOW!

"My Mother Is"

MY MOTHERS A VIOLET THAT BLOOMS FOREVER MORE.

SHE'S THE WISDOM AND BEAUTY OF THE MASTERS' LORE;

THE SPICE IN THE AIR ALONG A BEAUTEOUS SEASHORE;

THE PEACE UPON THE WATERS THAT THE MOON SHINES FOR!

BOUNTIFUL LOVE NEVER ENDING FROM HER HEART DOTH POUR;

WITH SOMEWHAT OF THE MISCHIEF AND AWE OF "LENORE."

IMAGIMATION AND WONDER SHE EVER HOLDS IN STORE;

PLUS ALL THE WARMTH AND BEAUTY BRAVE HEARTS DIE FOR!

POETRY AND BEAUTY MESHED WITH WISDOM AND MUCH MORE;

THOUGH SHE'S JUST "MY LITTLE MAMMA" I'M ENVIED FOR!

HER WAYS ARE QUAINT AND MODERN, NEVER A BORE;

HER HEART EVER WONDERS WHAT LIES 'LONG THE DISTANT SHORE:

HER LOVE SWEETLY REEMAINING IN ALL SHE'S TOUCHED BEFORE!

AND THOUGH I WISH I COULD KEEP HER WITH ME EVERMORE

SHE'S THE PRECIOUS GEM THAT THE BARD WRITES OF IN LORE.

NOT DOTH A VIOLET BLOOM BEHIND A CLOSED DOOR,

BUT POPS UP WHEN AND WHERE IT WHIST AND WHOM IT WHIST FOR!

P.S. AN EXOTIC GEM IS MUCH MORE PRECIOUS

WHEN UN-ED AND MUCH LONGED FOR!

THOSE WHO HAVE SEEN HER BEAUTY CAN HEAR A

GENTLE TAPPING AND FAINT CALL OF "LENORE."

"My Prayer for Direction"

DEAREST LORD JESUS DIRECT MY WAYS.

GIVE ME KNOWLEDGE TO FULFILL MY DAYS.

MAY THE SON SHINE, FOREVER IN MY HEART:

I NEED THY LIGHT INSIDE NOT TO FALL APART!

MY RESPONSIBILITIES ARE ENOURMOUS I KNOW

LORD HELP ME WITH THEM; THE MANY SEEDS TO SOW!

BE MY SUNSHINE AND DEW DROPS FOR GROWTH

SO I CAN BEFIT OTHERS WITH WHAT I KNOW!

"My Prayer for Your Health"

MAY THE LORDS' ANGELS ATTEND CLOSE TO THEE!

MAY THE FATHER ABOVE EASE YOUR PAIN AND QUICKLY
MAKE YOU WELL AGAIN!

MAY YOU FEEL THE WARMTH OF HIS COMFORTING, HAND.

MAY HIS BLESSINGS, AROUND YOU, BAND.

HE IS EVER CLOSE, HIS HELP IS EVER NEAR!

GIVE HIM YOUR PAIN TO COMFORT;

REACH OUT FOR HIS LOVING HAND!

MAY GOD BLESS AND KEEP THEE!

"My Requeim"

DEATH IS MERELY GOING ON HOME.

VERY OFTEN I WISH THAT PATH TO ROAM;

TO CROSS THE BLUE WATER, SO CRYSTAL CLEAR,

INTO ARMS OS JESUS; LOVED ONES DEAR!

NAY, DON'T CRY FOR ME WHEN I AM GONE:

TO WISH ME BACK IS BUT TO WISH ME WRONG!

MY LOVE WILL REMAIN WITH YOU EVER MORE

AS I DWELL ON THAT CELESTIAL SHORE!

"My Wish"

I WANT A LOVE FRAGRANT AS A ROSE,

A SWEET TRUE LOVE WHICH FOREVER GROWS.

PURE, WHITE, AS INNOCENT AS A DOVE:

TWO HEARTS, OVERFLOWING WITH LOVE!

I WANT A RING GIVEN WITH CARE

TO PROVE OUR LOVE WE DO SHARE;

A CHURCH WEDDING, A GOLD WEDDING BAND,

PLACED BY MY LOVE UPON MY HAND!

"My Youth"

MY YOUTH HAS FLED SOMEWHERE ALONG THE WAY,

CREEPING OUT OF MY LIFE SLOWLY, DAY BY DAY!

ONCE I MADE A TRUCE WITH A FRIEND OF MINE; FOREVER,

WE BOYH SAID; TRUE FRIENDSHIP WE DO BIND.

BUT I WAS A CHILD AND SINCE I HAVE LEARNED; FRIENDS

OFTEN ARE LOST, OR BY THEM YOU ARE SPURNED.

SO OUT CREPT MORE CHILDHOOD: AND THEN ENTERED,

MISTRUST! INNOCENT FAITH OF CHILDHOOD SPLINTERED!

NEXT, MY FAITH LAY IN TRUE LOVE; IT SEEMED BLISS.

THEN I FOUND TRUE LOVE FAULTY AT ITS' BEST!

MONEY USED TO BE SPECIAL, AN ADDED JOY. NOW IT'S

SOMETHING TO PINCH, NO LONGER A TOY!

I'M RAISING CHILDREN NOW AND WONDER WHY? IN

GROWING UP THEY'LL LEARN THIS JUST AS I.

THEN I REMEMBER, AS A CHILD OF THREE. I SAW

A BUTTERCUP BLOOMING; FOR ME!

LOOKING BACK AT MY PUPPY LOVES OF OLD, I RECALL

A MAGIC THAT WARMS WINTERS COLD!

THROUGH CHILDBIRTH I SAW I HAD BORNE THROUGH PAIN,

A LIFE TO MAKE ITS' MARK ON THIS WORLD OF MEN!

AND AS I WATCH MY CHILDREN GROW AND LEARN; AT

TIMES I JUST MAY FOR MY LOST CHILDHOOD YEARN,

BUT I SEE BEAUTIES OF THIS LIFE GIVEN, FROM OUR

"MOST HIGH" GOD LIVING UP IN HEAVEN!

BEAUTY LIES ON EARTH, THEM TO DISCOVER! I GAVE

THEM BIRTH, WHAT JOY TO BE A MOTHER!

166

"Nancy"

TURN AROUND, YOU WERE TINY
HAIR LONG AND HANGING DOWN.
TINY FACE, TINY HANDS, TINY FEET
WALKING THRU OUR BIG CROWDED TOWN!

TURN AROUND, AND YOU MET HIM,
STILL TINY, YET MY HOW YOU'D GROWN!
HEART BURSTING, SO FULL OF LOVE;
LOVE THAT ONLY IN YOUTH WE'VE KNOWN!

TURN AROUND, YOU HAVE CHILDREN.
MY, LOOK, LOOK HOW THEY GROW!
MY WOULDN'T IT BE BEAUTIFUL
TO KNOW WHAT THEY KNOW!

TURN AROUND MY LITTLE ONE, TURN,
FOR ALWAYS YOU'RE STILL THE TINY TOT.
FOR THIS MOMENT ONLY LET IT BE.
YOU'RE STILL A LITTLE ONE IN MY HEART!

"No More Tomorrow"

DO NOT LET ONE SMALL DAY SLIP BY
LEAVING A KIND WORD UNSPOKEN, A JOB UNDONE.
SOME TOMORROW YOU MAY BE LOST AS TO WHY
YOU COULDN'T HAVE HELPED THAT WANDERING ONE!

DO ALL YOU CAN FOR YOUR FELLOW MAN TODAY,
FOR THERE WILL BE NO MORE TODAY TOMORROW!
GOD WILL SHOW YOU PLENTY TO DO AND SAY,
HIS WORK FOR TODAY CANNOT WAIT E'RE SORROW!

DO NOT PUT IT OFF FOR OTHER WORK OR PLAY:
HE HAS NEW WORK FOR YOU EACH TOMORROW.
DO NOT LEAVE YOUR WORK UNDONE TODAY,
FOR THERE MAY BE NO MORE TODAY TOMORRROW!

"Nurses"

BLESS THE SWEET AIDS AND NURSES,
THER LACK OF CREDIDT IS SORE!
THEY ANSWER ALL OUR CALLS
AND TEND TO WHAT E'ER OUR NEEDS ARE!

THEIR SMILES ARE ALWAYS HEARTENING
ANSWERING EVERY TROUBLE EVERY NEED,
WATCHING O'ER US AS VERY ANGELS---
LO' ANGELS THEY SEEM TO BE INDEED!

REMEMBER TO GIVE THEM A BIG SMILE
AND ENCOURAGE THEIR HEARTS SOME TOO;
FOR THEIR HEARTS AND BACKS FEEL THE STRAIN
AND SOMETIME THEY BECOME BLUE!

IN THIS FAST DAY AND TIME WE PUT ASIDE
RESPECT FOR THE FLORENCE NIGHTINGALES OF TODAY.
THEIR HEART AND THOUGHTS ARE AS PURE AS GOLD!
AND THEY STAND GUARD IN SUCH AN ANGELIC WAY!

"Oak Tree"

WHEN I DIE, JUST BURY ME BENEATH A GIANT OLD OAK TREE:

PLANT VIOLETS WHERE I LAY.

IN THE SUMMER THE SUN SHALL SHINE O'ER ME.

IN THE FALL LEAVES SHALL SHOWER O'ER ME.

IN THE WINTER SNOW SHALL COVER ME.

FIREFLIES SHALL FLY O'ER ME IN THE DRK OF THE NIGHT,

TO MAKE MY RESTING PLACE SHINE BRIGHT;

MOTHER EARTH SHALL HOLD ME TIGHT!

PLANT YELLOW ROSES WHERE I LAY.

"Oh Which Way is Heaven"

WHERE DIDTHE MOON GET ITS' SILVERY LIGHT?

HOW DID THE STARS LIGHT UP THE BRK NIGHT?

WHERE DOES THE NIGHT GO WHEN MORNING COMES IN?

WHICH WAY IS HEAVEN AND WHERE GOES THE WIND?

HOW DOES THE WORLD TURN, DOES ANYONE KNOW?

WHY DOES A SEED DIE AND THEN START TO GROW?

HOW DOES A NEWBORN KNOW THINE MOTHERS HAND?

WHICH WAY IS HEAVEN AND WHRE GOES THE WIND?

YESTERDAYS' GONE, BUT WHERE DID IT GO?

TOMORROW MAY COME, BUT NOBODY KNOWS!

WHERE DOES THE LORD LIVE, OH WHERE IS THAT LAND?

WHICH WAY DID TIME GO AND WHERE GOES THE WIND?

CHORUS:

WONDERING WIND, WHISPERING WIND, WHERE ARE YOU GOING?

IS THERE NO WAY OF KNOWING? WHERE WILD WINDS ARE BLOWING?

WHICH WAY IS HEAVEN, WHERE GOES THE WIND?

WHICH WAY IS HEAVEN, WHERE GOES THE WIND?

"Orchid"

MY SISTER IS A PRECIOUS THING
A MELODY LIKE TINY SONG BIRDS SING:
LOVE AND LAUGHTER SHE EVER BRINGS.
SHE IS A PRETTY RAINBOW STRETCHING!

A MAGIC SHE SOMEHOW BESTOWS,
WITH A GENTLE KINDNESS, SHE OVER FLOWS!
WITHIN HER, AN ENDLESS WELL GROWS,
FILLING US WITH HAPPINESSS, HEAD TO TOE!

AN EXOTIC ORCHID, IS SHE,
A BEAUTY OF SWEET PERFECTION TO SEE!
WISE AND STRONG, GENTLE AS CAN BE;
SHE FLAUNTS EXOTIC BEAUTY PERFECTLY!

"Our Dear Jesus"

"OUR DEAR JESUS, HE NEVER EVER SINNED

YET THE POOR HELPLESS LEPER HE CLEANSED,

AND IT WAS OUR SWEET JESUS THEY SAID

THAT RAISED UP LAZARETH FROM THE DEAD!

IT WAS HE WHO CAME TO SET ME FREE......

AND SAID LET THE LITTLE CHILDREN COME TO ME.

"DO NOT HARM ONE OF THEM IN ANY WAY."

THE JUDGEMENT DAY WILL COME AND YOU WILL SURELY PAY!

HE GAVE ME HOPE, GOODNESS HE TAUGHT,

FOR HIS OWN COMFORT; NEVER GAVE A THOUGHT!

OUR JESUS MET THE WOMAN AT THE WELL.

HER LIFE STORY TO HER HE DID TELL.

HE OFFERED HER WATER TO QUENCH HER THIRST

IF SHE WOULD BELIEVE AND CHANGE HER WAY FIRST.

IT SADDENED HIM WHEN SOMEONE DIDN'T BELIEVE;

AND IN THE GARDEN, FOR ALL OUR SINS HE DID GRIEVE!

THEY TOOK OUR JESUS, THEY HURT HIM SO;

YET TO CLEANSE ALL OUR SINS HE CHOSE TO GO!

"Our Kylee Jo"

MY YOUNGEST GRANDAUGHTER IS KYLEE JO. HER
GREAT INTELLIGENCE SHOCKS ME.
LIKE MY MOTHER, SHE LOVES TO READ SO! IN
MANY WAYS SHE IS JUST LIKE ME.
SHE HAS A SWEET AND LOVING SMILE. SOMETIMES
WHEN SHE IS EXTRA GOOD
SHE'S IS SWEET AND SO PRECIOUS THE WHILE; AND
USES HER MANNERS LIKE SHE SHOULD!

WHEN I WAS GOOD, MY MOTHER OFTEN SAID JUST TO ME ALONE:
"THERE ONCE WAS A LITTLE GIRL WHO HAD A LITTLE
CURL RIGHT IN THE MIDDLE OF HER FORHEAD."
(SHE'D STOP TO PUSH AWAY MY LITTLE CURL, THEN ADD)
"WHEN SHE WAS GOOD, SHE WAS VERY, VERY GOOD
BUT WHEN SHE WAS BAD, SHE WAS HORRID!

I DIDN'T MIND THIS LITTLE VERSE, I LIKED IT VERY
WELL: FOR SHE SMILED A SWEET LOVING SMILE
AND I COULD SEE SHE MEANT TO TELL ME
TO ACK THAT WAY FOR AWHILE!
MY KYLEE IS LIKE ME! WHEN SHE IS GOOD; SHE
IS THE MOST PRECIOUS THING;
LIKE A PRINCESS OUT OF A STORY BOOK AND
I COULD GIVE HER ANYTHING!
BUT WHEN SHE IS BAD SHE IS …………..!

"Our Sydney"

SYDNEY HAS THE SWEETEST SMILE; A PERFECT SMILE!

TINY PINK FLOWERS BRING OUT HER DEEPEST SMILE.

SWEET AS BUTTERFLIES, SHE FLITS ABOUT ALL DAY;

SEEMS SHE WANTS FOREVER TO PLAY AND PLAY!

SHE GETS A BIT IMPISH, SHAKES HER BOOTY AT YOU:

AND DANCES, USING ALL THE LATEST MOVES.

SHE LEARNS QUICK, GAMES ARE HER FAVORITE TOO.

SHE LOVES TO WIN AND LESRNS HOW TO BEAT YOU!

SHE IS A BEAUTIFUL FLOWER IN MY GARDEN SO WIDE.

MY GARDEN OF GRANDCHIZZFBGFLDREN IS MY MAIN PRIDE!

SHE LOVES TEA PARTIES AND HOLDS HER PINKIE UP.

SHE LOVES TO ADD SUGAR LUMPS TO THAT TEA CUP!

SHE IS A QUICK LEARNER; SEEKS KNOWLEDGE WELL.

WHAT SHE WILL ONE DAY BECOME, IS HARD TO TELL.

BUT FOR NOW, SHE'S A HAPPY FIVE YEAR OLD,

LIVING FOR THE BEST OF EACH DAY AS SHE GROWS!

I LOVE YOU,

NANNY!

"Our Yellow Rose"

MEMORIES CAME CRASHING DOWN THROUGH MY MOTHERS MIND
OF THE HARD, SAD TIMES WE WENT THROUGH; WHEN I WAS YOUNG.
HURT OF MY DESTROYED HOPES AND DREAMS, WAS HURT THAT BINDS.
LIKE THE ROSE BUD; NIPPED E'ER BLOOMING; IT SLOWLY DIES:

MY HOPES OF HAPPINESS AND JOY WERE NIPPED, AND DIED.
I GREW VERY SERIOUS AND SELDOM DID SMILE,
I SELDOM LAUGHED; OFTEN WHEN ALONE I WOULD CRY.
MOTHER OFTEN BROUGHT ME A ROSE TO MAKE ME SMILE!

MUCH TIME HAS PASSED, MY DEAR MOTHER IN HEAVEN WAITS.
SAD TIMES ARE A MELONCHOLY MEMORY NOW.
MY DUGHTER OFT' BRINGS YELLOW ROSES IN A VASE.
SOMEHOW SHE HAS FOUND THAT THEY ALWAYS MAKE ME SMILE!

"Part of His Plan'

FROM THE SMALLEST BLOOMING FLOWER EYES SEE;

THROUGHOUT THE WHOLE OF OUR ENTIRE LAND;

MAN, GOD IN HIS OWN IMAGE MADE: WE

ALL ARE A PART OF THE MASTERS PLAN!

A FLOWER BLOOMS, BEAUTIFUL TO THE EYE,

BUT ALAS, THERE COMES A CERTAIN DAY

THE PRECIOUS BEAUTIFUL BLOOM, BY THE BY;

WILL START TO WANE, SLOWLY WILT AND FADE!

YET, DID NOT OUR DEAR GOD GIVE IT TO US

TO SEE THE BEAUTY, GIVE PEACE AND JOY!

AND IS NOT EACH FLOWERS BLOOMING JUST THUS

LIFE DECIDED; BY HIM, AS EACH GIRLS, EACH BOYS?

"TIS UP TO HIM WHEATHER THE BUD DOTH BLOOM;

'TIS UP TO HIM HOW LONG IT WILL GLOW!

'TIS THE SAME WITH MAN, AS HOW LONG, HOW SOON

WILL HE BLOSSOM, THEN WANE, WILT AND GO!

HE HOLDS ALL HIS OWN IN A SPECIAL WAY!

OUT OF KINDNESS THE WILTED, IN HIS HAND

HE CARRIES, THRU HEAVENS' SWEEET GOLDEN GATES!

TAKE COMFORT IN HIS BEAUTIFUL PLAN!

"Peace Be Still"

WHEN THE WATERS WERE TROUBLED JESUS SAID "PEACE BE STILL!"

THE RAGING WATERS FELL SILENT AND STILL AT HIS WORDS!

HE IS OUR "GREAT COMMANDER" OF ALL; THAT IS FOR REAL!

WHEN MY SOUL WAS OH SO HEART-BROKEN AND SO TROUBLED,

I HEARD THE SAME WORDS FROM UP HIGH, CLEARLY; "PEACE BE STILL!"

MY SOUL FELL CALM AT THOSE WORDS, FOR I KNEW THEY WERE REAL!

PRAYERS IN EARNEST, WHEN YOU HAVE FAITH, ARE ALWAYS ANSWERED!

PRAY THROUGH THE NAME OF JESUS, BELIEVING; "PEACE BE STILL!"

WHATEVER THE TROUBLE, IT WILL OBEY HIM E'EN NOW!

"PEACE BE STILL," THE COMMAND OF JESUS' IS EVER REAL!

"Peace that Flows"

THERE'S A PEACE THAT FLOWS LIKE A RIVER.

THE HOLY SPIRIT IS THE GIVER!

IT COMES FROM JORDANS OWN FOUNT IN HEAVEN;

BADE SENT FROM THE FATHER: TO US GIVEN!

I SAW THE FOUNT, MID HEAVENS' RIVER BLESSSED!

THE BEAUTY, THE POWER, THE SWEET HOLINESSS:

BREATH TAKING; SWEETER THAN WORDS OF MAN:

WITH PEACE GREATER THAN MANS' EXPRESSIONS!

"Please Don't Tell Me"

CHRISTIAN, PLEASE DON'T TELL ME; "THAT PERSON
DESERVED THE TABLES TO TURN!"
DON'T SAY; "OH, FOR THAT HE'LL BURN!" INSTEAD;
IN SORROW, GET DOWN ON YOUR KNEES!

NEVER SAY; "SEE, I TOLD YOU;" OR "OH, LET
ME TELL YOU THEIR LATEST SIN!"
PLEASE! FORBEAR CONDEMNING MEN. THE
"CREATOR SUPREME" IS YOUR JUDGE TOO!

CHRISTIAN, PLEASE DON'T TELL ME; "THEY'RE NOT
WORTH TAKING THE LORDS' GOSPEL TOO!"
THEY WOULD NOT LISTEN TO YOU? LET GOD'S
SAVING LOVE, THE DIFFERENCE BE!

NAY! DON'T TELL ME MENS' SIN! NAY; RELISH AT
WHAT YOU CALL DESERVED PAIN;
'LEST YOU HURT THAT ONE WHO CAME: SUFFERED
AND DIED; AROSE; FOR YOU AND THEM!

"Rady Dianna Bryant"

CHILD; YOU ARE A SWEET LITTLE FLOWER
A PRECIOUS LITTLE BLOOM OF GODS' LOVE.
GOD PICKED YOU FOR MOMMY AND DADDY
TO GROW; WHILE HE WATCHES FROM ABOVE!

GOD GIVES THE FLOWOERS RAIN AND SUNSHINE:
BUT HIS WONDERFUL LOVEE HE GIVES YOU!
AND HE PUT YOU IN A FAMILY ALL YOUR OWN
WHERE YOU HAVE A SPECIAL JOB TO DO.

YOUR JOB LITTLE ONE, IS TO LOVE AND GROW;
TO LISTEN GOOD; TO LEARN EACH AND EVERY DAY;
TO KEEP A PRETTY SMILE; 'TILL YOU ARE GROWN;
THEN SHOW OTHERS GODS' LOVE AND GODS' WAY!

"Rainbows and Unicorns"

RAINBOWS AND UNICORNS, LAUGHTER AMID LIFES' STORMS,

PREACE HOPE ALL THINGS TRUE LIVE INSIDE OF ME AND YOU!

IT'S A DREAM WE REACH FOR IN OUR MIND,

A DREAM OUR HEARTS AND MIND ENTWINE.

HAPPY COLORS, HAPPY DAYS, SWEET IMAGININGS

WITHIN THE SOUL, THROUGH OUR DREAMS; SURFACING.

RAINBOWS AND UNICORNS, LAUGHTER AMIID LIFES' STORMS

PEACE HOPE, ALL THINGS TRUE, LIVE I NSIDE OF M E AND YOU!

AH HE LOVES ME HE LOVES ME NOT

DAISIES KNOW, BUT THEY NEVER TELL WHAT!

OHH! ROSES ARE RED, VIOLETS ARE BLUE

RAINBOWS AND UNICORNS; LAUGHTER AMID LIFES' STORMS,

PEACE, HOPE ALL THINGS TRUE, LIVE INSIDE OF ME AND YOU!

AH! HE LOVES ME; HE LOVES ME NOT! DAISIES

KNOW BUT THEY NEVER TELL WHAT.

OHH! ROSES ARE RED, VIOLETS ARE BLUE; CAN WE

STILL BELIEVE THERE IS A LOVE SO TRUE?

RAINBOWS AND UNICORNS, LAUGHTER AMID LIFES' STORMS,

PEACE, HOPE. ALL THINGS TRUE LIVE INSIDE OF ME AND YOU!

THESE DREAMS WE REACH FOR IN OUR MINDS, THAT

THE MIND SURFACES THERE AND UNBINDS:

CAN REALLY FOR US "SEEM" BEAUTIFULLY TRUE; THE

SECRET IS IN JUST HOPING; FOR ME, FOR YOU!

RAINBOWS AND UNICORNS, LAUGHTER AMID LIFE'S STORMS,

PEACE, HOPE, ALL THINGS TRUE, LIVE INSIDE ME AND YOU!

"Reno Valley Sunrise"

THE NEON CLUB LIGHTS ARE A SPARKLING SIGHT

IN THE VALLEY OF RENO, LATE AT NIGHT!

ENTERTAINMENT AT ITS' FINEST ONE SEES

IN THIS GREAT CITY THAT NEVER GOES TO SLEEP!

THERE ARE SIGHTS TO SEE, THE CLUBS TO PLAY,

RESTAURANTS; FINE QUISINE BOTH NIGHT AND DAY!

BUT THE GREATEST SIGHT IS NOT MAN MADE AT ALL

AND GOES SO QUICKLY YOU MISS IT IF YOU STALL!

SMOKY BLUE MOUNTAINS WITH SNOW TOPS OF WHITE;

ENCIRCLE RENO; THE VALLY OF LIGHTS!

IN THE WEE HOURS ALL LOOKS GRAY BUT THE LIGHTS.

O'ER THE BLUE MOUNTAINS WITH RIDGES OF WHITE;

A FAINT GLOW, THEN COLOR EXPLOADS IN THE NIGHT!

ROSE, PINKS, BLUES, PURPLE! ABOVE RENOS' LIGHTS

WONDERS OF COLOR ARE A SWEET SURPRISE

RENO IS A NEON FOUNT MIDST A ROSE COLORED SUNRISE!

"Rose Colored Glasses"

JESUS' EYES WERE WIDE OPEN FOR HE CHOSE

TO SUFFER AND DIED FOR YOU:

SUFFERED MORE THAN ANY OF US CAN IMAGINE!

ARE YOU WEARING ROSE COLORED GLASSES?

FOR THERE ARE BUT TWO CHOICES:

TWO FORCES, "EVIL" AND "GOOD." YOU REAP

FROM ACTS YOU CHOOSE TO DO!

UNDERSTAND! THERE IS A CHOICE TO MAKE IN

THIS LIFE ON EARTH GOD MADE FOR YOU!

"YES, WHAT WILL YOU DO?" "THERE ARE TWO

FORCES WITH PLANS FOR YOU."

"DO YOU WALK BLIND, DESTINY UNKNOWN?" "OH! DO YOU NOT SEE?"

WITH EYES WIDE OPEN SATAN WISHED TO RULE HEAVEN WIDE AND

BE EQUAL WITH GOD. WHO CREATED ALL HEAVEN AND EARTH SO

WELL! HE BEGAN TO WAR WITHIN HEAVENS GOLDEN GATES! GOD

PUT HIM OUT OF HEAVEN AND CONDEMNED HIM TO HELL!

WITH EYES WIDE OPEN, JESUS TOLD JUDAS TO "DO WHAT YOU MUST

DO." JUDAS WOULD HAND HIM OVER TO BE CRUCIFIED HE KNEW! WITH

EYES WIDE OPEN, HE WENT WITH THE SOLDIERS SILENTLY; AND TOOK

THE BEATINGS, DERISION; WORE THE PAINFUL CROWN! WITH EYES

WIDE OPEN, HE TOOK LASHINGS FROM THE CAT O' NINE TAILS! WITH

EYES WIDE OPEN, HE WALKED AND CRAWLED GOLGATHAS' TRAIL!

WITH EYES WIDE OPEN, HE HEARD HIS MOTHERS' AND
LOVED ONES WAILS! WITH EYES WIDE OPEN, THEY NAILED
HIS FEET AND HANDS TO THE TREE! THEY SLASHED HIS SIDE;
THEY GAVE HIM VINEGAR TO DRINK FOR HIS THIRST! THEN,
WITH EYES WIDE OPEN, HE DIED FOR ALL HUMANITY!
BUT ONLY GOD HAS THE POWER OVER BOTH LIFE AND DEATH…
JESUS CAME BACK FROMTHE GRAVE ALIVE! GOD LEFT SATAN WITH
POWER TO VIE FOR MANS CHOICE OF GOOD OR EVIL: BUT NOT OVER
DEATH AND LIFE! WE HAVE TO CHOOSE BETWISEEN GOOD AND
EVIL; WITH EYES WIDE OPEN, I HOPE IT IS GOD YOU CHOOSE!
THERE IS A WHITE BOOK IN HEAVEN THAT WILL BE OPENED
JUDGEMENT DAY. THE NAMES OF ALL THOSE WHO HAVE 'BELIEVED'
WILL BE WRITTEN IN THAT BOOK AND READ THAT DAY. IF YOUR NAME
IS NOT LISTED THERE YOU WILL SPEND ETERNITY WITH SATAN.
BE SURE YOU CHOOSE WITH EYES WIDE OPEN,
NOT WITH ROSE COLORED GLASSES!

"Sara Demos"

SHE RELATED TO ME THE HISTORY OF HER NAME;
AND VERY CLOSE TO ADAM AND EVE IT CAME!

SHE OOOHED AND AHHED AND CROONED SOMETIME,
FOR OVER THE YEARS, MANY TALES HAVE ENTWINED!

HER NAMESAKE STEMS FROM THE BIBLE DAYS, ON.
SHE TOLD OF MANY WHO'VE COME AND GONE!

SHE LAUGHED AND COOED, SHE WAS VERY PROUD;
TO SPEAK OF SUCH AN HONOR TO ME; ALOUD.

THEN, SHE TOLD OF THE GREATNESS SHE'D LIVED UP TO;
THINGS THAT WOULD HONESTLY ASTOUND EVEN YOU!

SHE GRINNED, PONDERING THE GREAT THINGS TO COME,
AND I DOUBT NOT, SHE ACCOMPLISHES EVERY ONE!

"Searching"

SEARCHING, EVER SEARCHING,

FOR WISDOM AND A BETTTER ME.

STRIVING, EVER STRIVING,

FOR SUCCESS TO SET ME FREE.

DREAMING, EVER DREAMING,

OF HEAVENS OWN HOME FOR ME!

WAITING, EVER WAITING,

MY SWEET JESUS' FACE TO SEE!

"Seasons Passing"

LET ME BATHE IN A SUMMER BREEZE FROM THE FIELD;

LET MY SIGHT WANDER O'ER A FALLS HARVEST YIELD.

LET SNOW COVER MY WORLD ON A COLD WINTER'S EVE.

LET SPRING E'ER BLOSSOM, THAT I MAY CEASE TO GRIEVE!

MAY LIFES' HARDSHIPS AND TOILS; DISAPPOINTMENTS TRUE;

BE BAPTISED AND WASHED AWAY, WITH "SEASONS" ANEW!

MAY THE BLESSINGS OF NATURE, SURROUNDING ME O'ER;

WASH AWAY TROUBLES, AS THE SEA WASHES THE SHORE.

MAY MY JOY O'ER COME SIN AND SADDNESS HIDDEN;

MAY I GROW OLDER IN PEACE, IN THIS LAND GOD-GIVEN!

WHILE WE'RE YOUNG WE LIVE WITH NO PLAN FOR THE FUTURE;

WISER WITH AGE, THERE ARE MANY MISTAKES TO NURTURE.

NOT ALWAYS IS ONE'S LIFE WHAT ONE STROVE FOR IT TO BE:

MANY WRONG DECISIONS ONE CAN LOOK BACK AND SEE.

THE LAND COMES TO LIFE, GROWS, HARVESTS, DIES; AS DO WE.

I WISH TO BATHE IN ITS' "SEASONS" PASSING SO QUICKLY!

"Seeds of Kindnesss"

PLANT A SEED OF KINDNESS!

BE KIND TO SOMEONE YOU KNOW!

WATER IT OFTEN, FOR IT TAKES

REASSURANCE, FOR BEAUTY TO GROW!

AS THE SEED TAKES HOLD;

AND IN THE ROOT OF FRIENDSHIP HOLDS:

PLANT ANEW, IN OTHER SOILS.

PLANT MANY SEEDS! BE BOLD!

"Seek"

IF YOU SEEK GUIDANCE FROM GOD

BECAUSE YOU DON'T KNOW WHERE TO TURN;

IF KNOWLEDGE IS WHAT BECKONS YOU,

AND YOUR GREATREST WISH IS TO LEARN;

IF YOU SEEK THE GREATEST LOVE OF ALL,

IF YOU THINKIT CAN'T BE FOUND;

OR IF YOU WISH TO FIND INSTRUCTION:

THESE ARE ALL IN ONE BOOK, FANCILLY BOUND.

IF PEOPLE PERPLEX, HINDER OR CONFOUND YOU

OR YOU WANT JUST TO FIND A BETTER WAY;

IF YOU THINK SOMEWHERE THERE'S SOMETHING MORE:

PICK UP YOUR BIBLE, READ IT TODAY!

ANY PROBLEM YOU FIND AT HAND,

WHATEVER RACE, WHATEVER LAND;

THE BIBLE HAS AN ANSWER FOR YOU

IN LIFE AND AFTER…A BETTER LAND!

"Shields"

I WALK DOWN THE ROADSIDE, I WALK IN THE FIELDS.

I PASS MANY PEOPLE. THEY ALL CARRY SHIELDS!

WE CANNOT TRUST ONE ANOTHER, BROTHER OR FRIEND!

WE HIDE OUR EMOTIONS AND FEARS, WHERE WILL IT END?

WE DON'T KNOW WHAT TO BELIEVE IN, WHAT LEADER TO TRUST.

NO DOUBT, THE SAME LEADERS HOLD A BIT OF FEAR OF US!

AMERICA WHAT HAS HAPPENED, ONCE FULL OF LOVE SO FREE?

AMERICA, WE WANT YOU BACK LIKE YOU ONCE USED TO BE!

"AMERICA THE BEAUTIFUL," WHERE OUR FATHERS DIED;

WHERE PILGRIMS CRIED: WHERE PEOPLE STOOD SIDE BY SIDE.

"AMERICA, DEAREST AMERICA, WE MUST UNITE ONCE MORE;

E'ER OUR SOLDIERS WOULD EVEN KNOW WHAT TO FIGHT FOR!

"Simple Things, Wonderful Things"

WHEN SMALL, I OFT' LOOKED AT THE SKY, KNOWING GOD MADE IT!

THERE'S NO WAY MAN COULD HAVE CREATED THE HUGE SKY!

THE BIBLE PROVES PREDICTIONS YEARS PRIOR TO EVENTS. I

SAW THEY WERE PRECISE AS TO PLACE AND TIME-WISE!

I'VE SEEN RAINBOWS, SILVER LININGS; SUN RAYS THROUGH THE TREES.

FROM TOPS OF HILLS I'VE CLIMBED; I LET MY HAIR BLOW FREE!

I'VE SEEN MOUNTAINS OF ROCK SO MANY DIFFERENT HUES; A

FAVORITE THING; REDS, GOLDS, PINKS, PURPLES AND BLUES!

I HAVE SEEN DEATH VALLEY AND CHECKED OUT THE ALAMO:

WADED THE RIO GRAND, SAW LONE TUMBLE WEEDS BLOW!

I SAW A PICTURE OF NATURES PERFECTION: SURPRISE! BY A

CREEK COMING FROM THE KENTUCKY RIVER; WIDE:

ANOTHER TINY STREAM MADE ITS' WAY THROUGH A CLEARING,

ONLY ABOUT FIVE FEET SQUARE, 'MIDST WOODED TERRAIN.

'MID THE CLEARING WAS A TINY HILL WHERE THE STREAM

MADE A MINIATURE WATERFALL IN THE TINY GLADE!

THIS WAS ONE OF THE SWEETEST SIGHTS I HAVE EVER SEEN! I'VE

SEEN EASTERN KENTUCKY MOUNTAINS: THE SALT SEAS!

I HAVE SEEN THE BEAUTIFUL MOUNTAINS OF TENNESEE. I

KNOW THE SMOKY MOUNTAINS WAITED JUST FOR ME!

I SWAM IN LAKE ERIE, TAHOE AND THE OCEANS TOO. SAT

ON THE LONELY DOCK OF THE BAY, MISSING YOU!

I SAW GRAND CANYON AND NIAGARA FALLS. "BIRTH

OF A CHILD," BIRTH OF A CHRISTIAN;"

THE BEST SIGHTS OF ALL!

"Somewhere"

WERE E'ER THE SWEETEST ROSE DOTH GROW,

AND WHERE THE HIGHEST WAVE DOTH ROLL:

THERE IS A PLACE, YES I KNOW 'TIS "SOMEWHERE"

THAT GRASS GROWS GLEAMING IN THE SUN,

FLOWERS FLOURISH THERE!

FLOWING BEDS OF FLOWERS BREATHE SO FREE.

REACHING FOR THE SKY, IS EVERY TREE.

THE LIMBS HOLD SOFT TINY NESTS

OF CHIRPING BIRDS; SINGERS OF THE BEST!

I WISH I WAS THERE!

"Sow Seeds of Kindness"

YOU MAY DROP A SEED OF KINDNESS
AND NOT SEE THE PLACE WHERE IT FELL;
IT MAY GROW AND SOME POOR SOUL BLESS
OR TO SOME SOUL, THE GOSPEL TELL!

ONE NEVER KNOWS GOD'S BEST OF PLANS.
SOW AS YOU GO, LAND, AIR OR SEA,
GOD HOLDS THE OUTCOME IN HIS HAND,
OF WHAT YOU SOW; FOR EVE-RY SEED!

"Stephanie"

ONE OF MY LITTLE DUCKLINGS
JUST AS PRETTY AS COULD BE,
WANTED TO BE THE ONLY ONE;
BUT OTHERS: THERE WERE THREE!

I NEVER COULD SHOW I LOVED HER
QUITE ENOUGH YOU SEE:
AND IT HURT HER LITTLE FEELINGS
BECAUSE SHE HAD TO SHARE ME!

SO SHE STAYED EVER VERY NEAR
AND I STAYED EVER NEAR FOR HER.
WHENEVER WE WERE PARTED AT ALL,
WE MISSED WHERE THE OTHER WERE!

"Success Waits"

WHAT THE MIND CAN PERCEIVE AND THE EYE CONCEIVE,
MAN CAN ACHIEVE!

SUCCESS STANDS WAITING IN THE SHADOWS OF LIFES' LEAVES;
UPON THE SEEKERS AND DOERS, WHO MAKE GOALS AND BELIEVE!

OTHERS WHO STAND BY, JUST WAITING UPON SLY FATE'
GET CAUGHT IN A WEB OF FAILURE; TOO SOON IT'S TOO LATE!

GO SEEK OUT YOUR LIFES' DREAMS, MAKE THEEM COME TRUE!
DECIDE TO REACH YOUR GOALS, SUCCESS WILL COME OUT TO YOU!

"Sweet Sharon"

OUR SWEET LADY WITH A GEORGEOUS SMILE
YOUR JOYFUL PRESENCE IS CRAVED BY ALL!
SO GRACEFUL; YOU WITH YOUR HAT; STANDING TALL'
WITH YOU, DIGNITY VISITS AWHILE!

THERE'S NOT TIME TO SPEAK TO EVERYONE,
FOR ALL WANT SOME OF YOUR PRECIOUS TIME!
WITH SO MUCH TO SAY, TOO SOON TIME IS GONE,
TOO SHORT FOR A WORD; TOO SOON WE FIND!

MORE OF YOUR PRESENSE IS SURELY CRAVED!
WE HAVE MISSED YOUR PRESENCE ON SUNDAYS!
GET WELL, RETURN; ALL OUR HEARTS DO PRAY!
WE FEEL A LOSS WHEN YOU ARE AWAY!

"Tammy Sue Bryant"

YOUR EYES ARE THE COLOR OF SKY BLUE

YOU FOOT IS WAY TOO SMALL FOR A SHOE!

YOUR EBON BLACK HAIR MATCHES THE NIGHT

AND YOUR PRESENCE MAKES OUR WORLD SO BRIGHT

YOU'RE ONLY A TINY BABY GIRL,

YET BRING SUCH HAPPINESS TO OUR WORLD.

TAMMY SUE, LITTLE TAMMY, TELL ME TRUE

DID ANGELS ABOVE SEND US YOU?

YOU ARE SO TINY, SOFT AND SWEET;

LITTLE FINGERS, TINY TOES AND FEET;

SOFT AND WARM, COZY; A SLEEPY HEAD!

YOU ONLY WAKE WHEN TIME TO BE FED!

SO HELPLESS, TINY; OH JUST SO SMALL!

YOU SOON WILL LEARN TO TALK, AND TO CRAWL.

BUT TELL ME HOW SUCH A TINY THING

CAN BE SO PRECIOUS AND SUCH JOY BRING!

"Teens"

THEY ARE NOT TOO DIFFERENT; TEENS OF TODAY.
JUST LESSTEACHING LETS T A LOT MORE SWAY!

REALLY, WHO IS TO BLAME YOU CAN'T IN TRUTH SAY.
PARENTS HAVE NOT TAUGHT THEM OF GOD'S WAY!

DO YOU REMEMBER THAT SWEET INNOCENT SIDE
'NEATH THE BIG FRONT, THAT STILL THERE DOTH HIDE!

ALL THAT'S NEEDED IS FOR US TO LEND A HELPING HAND;
TAKE INTEREST AND SHOWLOVE TO THE TEEN BAND!

THEY CAN STILL BE SWAYED, WE MUST SWAY THEM;
FOR SATAN LURKS WITH SIN TO TEACH THEM!

HE WILL DRESS IT ANEW TO LOOK LIKE "THE THING;"
AND ANOTHER SOUL MAY TO HIM VICTORY BRING!
SO LEND A HAND TO THE WAYWARD IMPERTINENT YOUTH;
AND TEACH THEM GODS' WAY: THEY WILL NOT BE UN-COUTH!

"Tera Katherine"

OH PRECIOUS LITTLE NEICE OF MINE;

LITTLE TERA KATHERINE;

MAY GOD ABOVE YOUR DAYS BLESS

WITH SUNSHINE AND TENDERNES!

MAY ANGELS WATCH YOU SLEEP AT NIGHT,

AND SWEET DREAMS HOLD YOU EVER TIGHT!

I WISH YOU THE BEST OF FRIENDS AT PLAY;

LOVED ONES WITH YOU ON HOLLIDAY!

AND FOR THE TIMES YOU MUST BE ILL,

MAY THEY BE FEW AND SHORT, BY GOD'S WILL!

"Thank You Mamma"

JUST A LITTLE GIRL WITH DREAMS

DAISIES, VIOLETS, CLOVER AND THINGS:

IN A WORLD FULL OF TROUBLES

AND OH SO MANY BURST BUBBLES!

"THANK YOU MAMMA"

FOR EVER KEEPING MY DREAMS ALIVE

AND EVER SHOWING ME THE PRETTY SIDE."

A LITTLE GIRL SO VERY HARD TO REACH,

BUT ALWAYS EAGER TO HAVE YOU TEACH!

"THANK YOU MAMMA"

GOD BLESS LOVE FOR DAISIES AND VIOLETS WILD

AND ALL THE LOVE YOU PUT IN THIS CHILD!

FOR GOD HAS BLESSED AND FILLED HER CUP

BY ANSWERING HER DREAMS AS SHE GREW UP!

"THANK YOU MAMMA"

HAPPINESS IS JUST LOVE I HAVE FOUND;

TOPPED WITH NATURAL BEUTY ALL AROUND!

A LOVING HEART GROWS BEST WHEN GIVEN

TO A CHILD FROM MOTHER AND GOD IN HEAVEN!

"THANK YOU MAMMA"

YOU DID YOUR PART!

"The Broken Shells of America"

YOUNG AMERICA FOR HER FREEDOM FOUGHT;

A FLAG WAS DESIGNED BY BETSY ROSS.

MANY BRAVE SOLDIERS MARCHED OFF; THE BATTLE

WAS WON: BLOOD SHED; LIVES LOST!

ALONG THE SHADOWS, ACROSS THE HILLS THE TEARS

OF WIVES, MOTHERS, CHILDREN; LEFT CHILLS!

THE WOUNDED FAMILIES OF SOLDIERS PRAYED;

AMERICAS' BROKEN SHELL RELAYED!

YOUNG AMERICA ONCE AGAIN FOUGHT. OFT' BROTHER

AGAINST BROTHER: MANY LIVES LOST.

SLAVES BADLY NEEDED TO BE SET FREE! THE

LOSS TOOK ITS TOLL PITIFULLY!

ALONG THE SHADOWS ACROSS AMERICAN HILLS TEARS

OF BLACK AND WHITE FAMILIES LEFT CHILLS!

SO GREAT WAS THE LOSS AMERICA IS STILL

STRIVING TO HEAL THE BROKEN SHELL!

THEN CAME WORLD WAR ONE; MANY SOLDIERS WENT

OVER SEAS; FOUGHT IN MANY COUNTRIES!

AGAIN WE WON! MANY MEN BLED, DIED. YET, THEY

FOUGHT FOR OUR LAND; WE HAD PRIDE!

STILL; LYING IN SHADOWS ACROSS THE HILLS, THE TEARS

OF WIVES, MOTHERS; CHILDREN LEFT CHILLS!

THE BROKEN SHELL OF AMERICA, WITH LOVE

AND PRAYER WAS SOON TO HEAL!

THEN CAME WORLD WAR TWO. WE WERE ATTACKED.
WE QUICKLY ROSE; RALLIED TO THE CALL!
MANY BRAVE SOLDIERS LEFT BY AIR; BY SEA. WE WON!
STILL MANY DIED OR WERE WOUNDED!
ALONG THE SHADOWS, ACROSS THE HILLS, THE TEARS
OF WIVES, MOTHERS; CHILDREN LEFT CHILLS!
WAR HAD BROUGHT MACHINERY, WE WORKED; WE
HAD HOPE: QUICKLY THE SHELL WAS HEALED!

"The Broken Shell of Americas' Shame"

MY HIGH SCHOOL SENIOR YEAR, A USELESS,

HOPELESS POLITICAL WAR CAME ABOUT!

BOYS JOINED, BOYS WERE DRAFTED: MY HEART

BROKE TO SEE HOPE OF AMERICA WASTED!

WE WANTED TO CLEAN UP THE WATER AND THE

AIR, TO DO WHAT MOST MATTERED!

THEY WOULD HAVE QUICKLY WORKED ON GLOBAL

WARMING! WE HAD KENNEDY'S HOPES.

WE HAD HIGH IDEALS FOR AMERICA....HIGH

IDEALS LIKE KENNEDY HAD HAD!

BUT THEY WERE SENT; OUR YOUNG MEN, TO DIE;

FOR A WAR WE COULD NOT WIN: ON A LIE!

ONE AND ONE HALF MILLION MEN DIED IN

A WAR WE HAD NO BUSINESS IN!

A POLITICAL WAR WE COULD NOT WIN BUT WOULD BRING MONEY IN!

"SO"

IN VIET NAM OUR YOUNG BOYS WENT TO WAR:

NOT TO KEEP AMERICA SAFE: WHAT FOR!

IT WAS A HORRIBLE WAR! MANY WERE KILLED

BY LITTLE CHILDREN; BOYS, GIRLS.

IF THEY ONCE HESITATED TOO LATE! WHAT KIND

OF PEOPLE HAD THIS MUCH HATE?

ALONG THE SHADOWS, ACROSS HILLS, TEARS OF

WIVES, MOTHERS; CHILDREN LEFT CHILLS!

THEN: WHEN THE MEN STRAGGLED HOME, INJURED
PHYSICALLY, OR/PERMANENT NIGHTMARES OF HORROR:
THEY RECEIVED NO RESPECT NOR PRIDE: THEY
WERE DERIDED OR JUST PUT ASIDE!
THEY PUT UP A MEMORIAL…TOO LATE FOR MOST
OF THEM TO SEE THEIR NAME ON A WALL.
ALONG THE SHADOWS ACROSS THE HILLS, ALL
WHO REALLY CARED LEFT CHILLS!
THE BROKEN SHELL OF AMERICA AFTER FIFTY YEARS LIES UN-ATONED.
THERE IS STILL A CHILL FROM WHICH AMERICA MAY NEVER HEAL!

"The Child in Me"

SOMETIMES I FLEE TO HIDE AWAY IN A CHILDS' LITTLE WORLD:

AT TIMES IT HAS BEEN SAID; "SHE ACTS LIKE A LITTLE GIRL."

AS A MATTER OF FACT I REFUSE TO GROW SO ADULT THAT I

LOSE TRACK OF THE GIRL INSIDE: "I WON'T GROW UP!"

LIFES' TRIALS GROW VERY HEAVY: LIFE'S DECISIONS OFT' HARD:

LIFES' BURDENS DWINDLE, WHEN I PICK CLOVER IN THE YARD!

IT REMAINS A PLEASURE THAT CLOVER, A SWEET NECKLACE MAKES;

IN A CHILDS' LOVELY WORLD OF SEEING WHAT GOD CREATES!

NO WORRIES OR BURDENS, JUST A SMILE, THEN, "I LOVE YOU:" FOR

ALL A CHILD ASKS OF THE WORLD IS; "PLEASE LOVE ME, DO!"

SO, OFTEN I FLEE TO THAT WORLD, LEAVING BURDENS AND CHORES;

TO FIND THAT BLISSFUL WONDER KNOWN WHEN A LITTLE GIRL!

GROWN UP THINGS MUST WAIT ON HOLD; UNTIL I RETURN AGAIN:

THEY WILL FALL IN PERSPECTIVE, AS CHILD AND WOMAN BLEND!

WEARY BURDENS WILL LINE OUT, A CLEARER VIEW WILL I SEE; WHEN

I RETURN FROM THAT WORLD, "THE LITTLE CHILD IN ME!"

OH HOW WOND'ROUS TO GET AWAY FROM ALL THAT WORIES YOU: SMILE

AND GREET THE WORLD WITH; "I LOVE YOU, PLEASE LOVE ME, TOO!"

THE PUREST, SWEETEST LOVE LIES IN INNOCENT YOUTH, THEN FADES!

I'LL EVER STAY IN TOUCH WITH THAT PRECIOUS WORLD GOD GAVE!

"The Dawn of Warning"

ALL THROUGH THE NIGHT THE RAIN POURED!

LIGHTNING FLASHED! THUNDER ROARED!

THE NIGHTS' COAT OF DARKNESS ADJOURNED,

THE BLACK CLOUDS WAYWARD TURNED!

BIRDS SWEET SONGS SOARED TOWARD HEAVEN, HIGH.

THE MIGHTY SUN PEEPED FROM THE SKY!

IN THAT INSTANT; WHAT GLORY I DID LEARN:

I SAW GODS' WRATH TO SWEETNESS TURN!

'MIDST THE BEAUTY OF IT ALL, THE QUESTION CAME;

"HOW LONG WILL HIS MIGHTY WRATH, HE TAME!"

"WE HAVE TRIED HIS PATIENCE O'ER AND O'ER:

WILL HE PROLONG HIS COMING VERY MUCH MORE?"

"UPDATE: 45 YRS LATER"

SIN IS RAMPID, THINGS HAVE WORSENED SO MUCH MORE!

AND FOR WORSE THINGS, THEY EVER SEARCH FOR!

OFT' I HEAR THUNDER ROAR: LIGHTNING CLASH!

SIN IS LIKE SODOMS'; HOW LONG CAN EARTH LAST?

1970 (UPDATE: MARCH 2015)

"The Faded Rose"

THE PETALS OF THE ROSE REACHED TOWARD THE SKIES!

LIFE, COLOR AND WARMTH LIVED INSIDE THE ROSE.

IT BEAUTIFULLY ADORNED THE YOUNG GIRLS' HAIR,

BRINGING OUT THE DEEP PURE BEAUTY FROM HER EYES.

THE ROSE WILTED AND TURNED PURPLE IN IT'S VASE;

SO LIMP, SO LIFELESS! DEAD AND WITHERED; YET IT STILL

DID NOT BRING A FROWN UPON THE YOUNG GIRLS' FACE!

AS SHE REMEMBERED, IT BROUGHT A SWEET, LOVING SMILE!

THE ROSE, PRESSED IN THE BIBLE, IS NOW CRISP AND YELLOW.

THE GIRL, MUCH OLDER, WISER; TREASURES THE MEMORY

OF THE YOUNG MAN WHO GAVE IT SO MANY YEARS AGO.

AH, SO IN LOVE: YEARS NOW GONE; HE LIES LIFELESS TOO!

SEEING THE RED DEWY, PETALS ALIVE AND BRIGHT;

THEY'RE FILLED WITH THE AROMA OF SWEETNESS AND LOVE:

I DARE SAY, THEY MEAN MORE TO GRANDMOTHER TONIGHT

THAN HER HALF EATEN, HALF FORGOTTEN…………...…SUPPER!

"The Gospels"

MATHEW, MARK, LUKE, JOHN; APOSTLES

OF OUR JESUS; GODS' ONLY SON.

THEY FOLLOWED JESUS HIS LAST YEARS

THEY KNEW HIS STORY AND HIS TEARS!

MATHEW, MARK, LUKE, JOHN, THEY WROTE BOOKS;

FOUND IN THE BIBLE. YOU SHOULD LOOK!

THEY TELL THE LIFE STORY OF JESUS.

LIKE NO OTHER: WRITTEN FOR US!

MATHEW, MARK, LUKE, JOHN, THEY ALL TELL

WHY GOD SENT HIM HERE, TELL IT WELL.

HE WAS SENT TO DIE ON THE CROSS

IN ATONEMENT FOR OUR SINS

MATHEW, MARK, LUKE, JOHN, WILL TELL HOW.

HE DIED; CAME BACK ALIVE: IN HEAVEN NOW!

THERE'S MUCH MORE; WORLDS GREATEST STORY!

MATHEW, MARK, LUKE; JOHN: BOOKS ARE GLORY!

"The Greatest Play"

THE CUTAIN FALLS FOR THE GREATEST PLAY E'ER WRITTEN:
STRANGELY ENOUGH, THE PLAY IS JUST MANS' HISTORY
WHEN THE VERY FIRST CURTAIN FALLS YOU WILL WITNESS
BLACKNESS! SOLID BLACKNESS, FOR FIRST THERE IS NOTHING!

THEN BEGINS CREATION; THE PLAY IS SEVEN ACTS LONG.
THEN HISTORY COMES, FOLLOWED DOWN THROUGH TIME!
SO MANY ACTS, SO MANY GREAT HEROES COME ALONG!
MOSES SETTING THE SLAVES FREE IS A FAVORITE OF MINE.

THERE ARE STORIES OF WARS WITH MORE HEROES TO TELL.
THE ACTS CONTINUE; HISTORY UN-FOLDS IN SECTIONS
STORY AFTER STORY FINALLY ACTS OF JESUS OWN LIFE
THEN STORIES OF HIS CRUCIFICTION AND RESURRECTION.

FINALLY COMES PREDICTIONS OF THE END OF THIS WORLD!
THE STORY OF EARTH AND MAN TOLD ACT AFTER ACT!
THE GREATEST PLAY WITH ACTS OF MAN, GOD; WORLD!
FROM THE BEGINNING TO THE VERY LAST ACT: TRUE FACTS!
TO BE CONTINUED: IN HEAVEN!

"The Hour Before Dusk"

ONE HOUR BEFORE DUSK AS THE SUN SHINES LOW

SHADOWS FALL HEADLONG AND LIFE BEGINS TO SLOW.

SOUND CARRIES FROM A FARTHER DISTANCE. NOW IS WHEN

I LOVE TO LAZE AND LISTEN TO DAYS APPROACHING END;

FOR YOU CAN HEAR THE DAY SLOWLY BEGINNING TO CLOSE.

SOFTLY IN THE BEGINNING, SHADOWS WILL COOL THE ROSE.

BUSY CHILDREN SEEM TO QUIET THERE NOISY PLAY

AND THE QUIET PEACE OF EXPECTANCE CALMS THE HECTIC DAY!

IT'S TIME FOR SWEET REST 'ERE THE SETTING OF THE SUN,

THE BEAUTIFUL SWEET HOUR BEFORE DUSK HAS BEGUN.

THERE IS BEAUTY IN SEASONS; DAWN, DUSK AND NOON:

BEAUTY IN WARM DAYLIGHT AND IN COOLNESSS OF THE MOON.

YET, TOO 'OFT IS LOOKED OVER THIS HOUR, COMING BEFORE DUSK;

AND I JUST WANT TO THANK YOU LORD FOR MAKING IT THUS!

MAN CAN LAZE AND LISTEN TO NIGHT FALLING SOFT AND SLOW;

ENJOY DAYLIGHTS LAST GLIMMER; FULLNESS OF ITS' BEAUTY KNOW!

"The Intangible Childhood Picture"

HOVERING OVER TODDLERS ON AN OLD DECAYED BRIDGE;

WAS AN ANGEL WITH HUGE WHITE WINGS: GUARDING OVER

A BROTHER AND SISTER WHO MIGHT TODDLE O'ER THE EDGE!

I KNEW GOD HAD SENT THE ANGEL TO CARE FOR THE BABES:

THE ANGEL SEEMED MOTHERLY AND WAS BEAUTIFUL!

SHE HAD THE SWEETEST, PUREST AND MOST CONFIDENT FACE.

FIRST I WAS CONCERNED AT SUCH A PRECARIOUS PLACE;

THE ANGELS PICTURE SOOTHED AWAY ANY SUCH FEARS.

I NOTICED THE PICTURED FOILAGE AROUND THE OLD BRIDGE.

ONLY IN A PAINTING COULD THRIVE SUCH FOILAGE!

I WAS ABOUT FIVE YEARS OLD AND IMPRESSED WITH PICTURE.

ONCE IN A GREAT WHILE I'D SEE ANOTHER COPY.

NOW I SEE THEM OFTEN, BUT IT IS NEVER THE SAME!

I SEE THE PAINTING BUT DON'T KNOW THE ARTISTS' NAME.

IF ADULTS COULD LOOK THROUGH CHILDRENS' EYES; THE BEAUTY SEE

THAT THE YOUNG AND INNOCENT EYE ALWAYS DOTH SEE;

THEY WOULD THEN AND ONLY THEN BE OLD AND ALSO WISE:

THEY APPRECIATE ALL AS A BRAND NEW GREAT SURPRISE!

"The Lonely Seagull"

WHERE THE WAVES ROLL UP FROM THE DEEP SEA

ARE MEMORIES OF WHEN I WAS SIXTEEN!

LONG AGO ON YON' SHORE ONE EBON NIGHT, A SEAGULL,

WITH AWESOME BEAUTY, TOOK ITS FLIGHT.

THE SKY LOOMED LIKE A DARK SHEET OF SPACE: MOONLIGHT

FELL IN SOFT FOLDS; LIKE GOLDEN DRAPES.

O'ER THE MOON SAT SPRINKLES OF TWINKLING STARS.

A YELLOW ONE SOMEONE SAID, WAS PLANET MARS.

LOOKING UP FROM THE WARM SHORES OF SAND, I

FELT SO SMALL, AWED BY OCEAN AND LAND.

FROM HER DRAPED GOLDEN FOLDS, THE MOON THAT NIGHT

SENT SHIMMERING RAYS, TIPPING THE WAVES WITH LIGHT.

ROLLING WATERS WASHED THE CRYSTAL BEACH, WATER

AND SAND BOTH BLENDED; MOONLIGHT BLEACHED:

THEN FADED INTO THE SKIES MASSIVE SPACE. VAST, DARK,

OCEAN AND SKY: SHOWED NO PARTING PLACE!

LIKE TRUE LOVERS THEEY BLENDED AS ONE, NO

LINE OF SEPERATION; THERE WAS NONE!

THEIR LOVE BEAT TO A MYSTERIOUS CALL: NOISE FROM

PULSING WAVES, PERMEATED SKY AND ALL!

THE MOON STILL SENT HER SILVERY RAYS: WHENCE

CAME A NEW SOUND.....AND A FLASHING TRACE

OF MOVEMENT OVER THE WATER.....I HEARD A SUDDEN

SPLEASH.....THE DARK WATER......DISTURBED.

A LONE GULL WINGED SILENT THROUGH THE NIGHT…..

DOVE FOR A FISH, IN THE EBON MOONLIGHT.

BARELY A BLUR…..SHE GLIDED SWIFT AND FREE… …NEVER

KNOWING THE BEAUTY; GOD HAD HER LEAVE FOR ME!

"The Lord Dropped Seeds to Guide Me"

MY GRANDMOTHER ASKED THE LORD'S HELP

WITH THINGS ALL DAY LONG.

SHE'D PRAY FOR US IF WE WERE SICK; AND IF WE DID WRONG;

SHE'D TELL US TO ASK FOR GODS' FORGIVENESS WHEN WE PRAYED.

I GUESS SHE SOWED MOST SEEDS THE LORD SENT FOR ME THOSE DAYS.

I CRAVED BEAUTY SO. THE LORD HAD MY COUSIN SHOW ME

A YARD WITH SPRING BUTTERCUPS, A GREAT PLEASURE FOR ME!

WHEN I WAS FIVE, MISSIONARIES CAME WITH SONGS AND GIFTS;

A GREAT LESSON FOR A YOUNG SPIRIT NEEDING A LIFT!

WHEN SEVEN A NEIGHBOR SAW I LIKED BUTTERCUPS WELL.

SHE TALKED TO ME AND SAID THEIR REAL NAME WAS DAFFODILLS.

SHE SENT ME TO CAMP WITH HER NIECE WHEN I WAS AGE NINE;

ASKED ME OVER ONCE FOR STRAWBERRIES AND CREAM....DIVINE!

ONE NEIGHBOR ASKED ME TO BIBLE SCHOOL, WHERE I WAS SAVED!

MY YOUNGER BROTHER WAS SAVED TOO, THE VERY SAME DAY!

ALL THESE SEEDS WERE DROPPED BY SOWERS THE LORD SENT SEEDS TOO.

HE SENDS SEEDS TO BE SOWN EVERY DAY. SOMETIMES THEY

GET SOWN WHERE GOD SENDS THEM, SOMETIMES

THEY'RE DROPPED BY THE WAY.

IF ONE IS NOT SOWN AN IMPORTANT LESSONS' UNLEARNED.

PLEASE STOP AND HELP THAT PERSON ALONG YOUR LIFE'S HIGHWAY:

THE SEED SOWN MAY ENCOURAGE; OR SAVE SOMEONE TODAY!

"The Pastors Wife"
(DEDICATED TO SANDY WALKER; WHAT A WORKER!)

TO THE WOMAN WHO STANDS BESIDE THE PASTOR,
DOES THE TASKS THAT CLEAR A PATH FOR HIM EACH DAY.
SHE STANDS BEHIND THE SCENES, WORKING FOR
ALL OF US SMOOTHING OUT SO MANY WAYS!

SHE TOILS AND GIVES HER ALL TO HELP HIM FULFILL HIS CALL.
THE LORD ABOVE SEES EACH EFFORT, SEES ALL SHE GIVES.
HE CHERISHES ALL OF HIS DAUGHTERS CARE FOR US ALL,
AND THE PASTOR; FOR THE CHURCH, FOR TIME SHE GIVES!

SHE DOES NOT ASK FOR RECOGNITION, OR THANKS.
SHE JUST NATURALLY GIVES A HELPING HAND.
HER JOB IS ENDLESS; NOT MANY UNDERSTAND!
YET SHE MARCHES ON FOR GOD AND HUSBAND.

SHE IS PRICELESS!

"The Pot of Gold"

I FONCE OUND A RAINBOW, OH SO GAY AND BRIGHT;
EXCITING; SO MANY DIFFERENT COLORED LIGHTS!

I REACHED OUT AND TOUCHED A GOLDEN HUE,
THEN ANOTHER, THEN ONE RED, YELLOW, BLUE.

A THOUSAND DIFFERENT COLORS FADING TOGETHER;
GOD PUT THEM THERE TO SEE, I GATHER.

BUT THEN ONE DAY MY RAINBOW BEGAN TO FADE,
THEN COMPLETELY DISAPPEARED I'M AFRAID.

I SEARCHED AND SEARCHED FOR MY PRETTY RAINBOW,
I WONDERED IF IT WERE REALLY REAL, I HAD TO KNOW.

THEN ONE DAY WHILE SEARCHING DOWN A LITTLE ROAD,
I CAME UPON AN ENOURMOUS POT OF GOLD.

PERHAPS MY RAINBOW IS FOREVER LOST IN THE SEA,
BUT IT LEFT ANOTHER GIFT, ONLY FOR ME!

"The Rose"

THE ROSE IS ONE OF GOD'S WONDERS
PERFECT ARE THE BUD, THE PETALS; BLOOMS!

THE ROSEBUD IS WRAPPED SO TIGHTLY
THE SMALL PETALS ALL EVENLY MADE.

WHEN THE ROSE OPENS, EACH PETAL
PARTIALLY COVERS THE VERY NEXT.

THE ROSE IS ALL IN UNISM
FROM TINY BUD TO THE PETALS BLOOM!

MORE, THE PETALS ARE VELVET SOFT.
COULD ANYTHING BE ANY SOFTER?

THEN THE HEAVENLY AROMA
NONE SWEETER THAN BEDDS OF ROSES!

ONLY GOD COULD HAVE MADE THE ROSE!
ONLY HE CAN MAKE SUCH PERFECTION!

"The Sea, Home"

I MUST GO BACK TO THE SEA ONCE MORE.

'TIS WHAT MY HEART IS LONGING FOR.

I MUST RETURN TO THE SANDY BEACH,

WHERE NATURE FEELS WITHIN MY REACH.

HOME, SWEET HOME; SO BEAUTIFUL TO ME.

I MUST GO AGAIN, GO TO THE SEA!

OH THE WAVES, THE SAND, AND STARRY SKY:

HOME WHERE THE MANY SEAGULLS FLY.

MY HOME IS CALLING ME BACK AGAIN;

I WANT TO FEEL MY FEET IN THE SAND!

'TIS ONE OF THE GREATEST PLEASURES, THIS;

TO BASK WHERE GOD CREATED SUCH BLISS!

"The Touching Sermon"

OUR PASTOR PREACHED A WAY OF FORGIVENESS

FOR EACH BRETHRENS' ERRORS AND SINS.

HIS SERMON PAINTED A BEAUTIFUL PORTRAIT

SHOWING SALVATION FOR ALL, DEAR OR KIN!

AND TEARS FLOWED TO MY EYES

AS THE BRETHREN SO FEW, SAT THERE.

FOR JUST A SMALL HANDFUL WERE WE

AND SO MANY NEEDED GODS' CARE!

WHAT MUST WE DO LITTLE HNDFUL OF MEN?

GODS' WORDS ARE TAUGHT EACH SERVICE ANEW.

THEY CANNOT BE IN VAIN, BRING PEOPLE IN!

UPON FAITH WE MUST BUILD AND FILL EACH PEPW!

PRAY FOR INCREASE IN THE LORDS' CREW.

CCOME TO ALL SERVICES, GOD NEEDS YOU!

WHEN YOU COME, INVITE A FRIEND,

AND WORK TO BRING A LARGE FAMILY ALL IN

"The Tree and Me"

THE TREE......"WHO ARE YOU GIRL?" "WHY ARE Y
PERHAPS MY RAINBOW IS FOREVER LOST IN THE SEA,
BUT IT LEFT ANOTHER GIFT, ONLY FOR ME!
OU HERE?" "YOU THERE, WALKING THE GARDEN WIDE."
"PERHAPS IT'S THE MACHINE YOU FEAR." "DID
YOU COME HERE ONLY TO HIDE?"

GIRL......"NO, NO!" "IT WAS NOT FEAR BEAUTY
CALLED ME IN TO SEARCH FOR THE ROSE."
"I'LL FIND WHICH PETALS CLAIM TO BE THE
SOFTEST VELVET; THESE. OR THOSE!"

THE TREE......"BEAUTY?" "WHY THIS CANNOT BE TRUE."
SOMETHING GREATER: SUCH AS THE SEA
SURELY WAS CALLING OUT TO YOU!" "THE GREAT
SEA IS WHERE YOU SHOULD BE!"

GIRL......"OH NO TREE, IT IS HUGE AND GREEN!"
"I CRAVE SERENE BEAUTY!" "THE ROSE
HAS GREATER BEAUTY TO BE SEEN." "EACH
HOLDS WONDER IN PERFECT POSE!

"THE TREE......" AH, YES." "YOU WERE BECKONED
HERE, TRULY NOT TO THE HUGE GIANT SEA!"
NO, NOT HIDING' BUT SEEKING DEAR, FOR A PERFECT SERENE BEAUTY!"

GIRL......"DEEP AND DARK WAS THE STRANGLING SEA!"
"THE SOFT ROSE; PURE, GENTLE AND TRUE."
"THE SEA OF HARSHNESS CLUTCHED AT ME!" "THERE'S
PEACE AND BEAUTY HERE WITH YOU!"

"The Web of Life"

THE WEAVING OF A WEB TAKES VERY LITTLE TIME IT SEEMS.

ALTHOUGH MAN SPINS AND WEAVES IN ALL

HIS MANY HOPES AND DREAMS!

"LIFES' WEB IS: IDEALS, HOPES, MORALS, AND DECISIONS MADE.

TO WEAVE ALL THESE INTO A "WEB OF LIFE," MAN WORKS AND SLAVES!

HE MAKES MISTAKES, THEN PATCHES THE WEB BACK HERE AND THERE;

TRYING VAINLY, TO KEEP HIS SPUN THREADS IN TACT EVERYWHERE!

"TIS FUNNY, THIS SLOW WEAVING OF WEBS; DONE BY MERE MEN:

WEAVING SLOW AND HARD TO PUT EACH ORIGINAL WEB IN;

FOR A GUST OF WIND WILL COME: ONE DREAM WILL BE GONE!

BROKEN IS THE HARD SPUN THREAD. BUT ONCE AGAIN, MAN WEAVES ON!

ONE BY ONE, MANY THREADS ARE BROKEN, THEN BLOWN AWAY.

GONE ARE THE TINY FIIBERS, IDEALS; HOPES, OF YESTERDAY!

TRYING TO MEND EACH NEW BROKEN FIBER, ONE BY ONE;

IT ALMOST BREAKS THE HEART, STILL; MAN CONTINUES TO WEAVE ON!

VERY SOON THE ORIGINAL "WEB OF LIFE" IS LOST:

ALTERED WHILE MENDING ALL THE DAMAGE LIFES' WEATHER HAS COST!

AFTER ALL THE HEARTACHE AND MENDING, PLUS SLOW HARD WORK'

MAN WONDERS IF ALL THE SPINNING ONLY LEAVES "PATCHED UP HURT."

THINKING THE SIMPLE ORIGINAL BEAUTY ALL GONE,

MAN SLOWLY TURNS TO SEE THE RESULT OF WHAT HE HAS SPUN.

TURNING; HE SEES BEAUTIFUL CHORDS OF SILVER AND GOLD

ALONG ALL THE LINES HE HAD MENDED FROM: LIFES: WIND AND COLD!

"The Wisdom of a Child"

"CHRISTIAN, WHAT ART THOU?" "DOST THOU KNOW?"
"YES, FATHER. I AM A BANKER, I'VE LONG BEEN SO."

"REMEMBER ASKING YOUR SON, WHAT HE WOULD BE?"
"YES FATHER," HE ANSWERED: "WHAT IS BEST FOR ME?"

"CHRISTIAN, COULD YOU NOT HAVE ANSWERED ME THUS?"
"UNLIKE THE CHILD, IN ME YOU DO NOT HAVE ENOUGH TRUST!"

"THE YOUNGEST CHILD TRUSTS HIS PARENT TO BE WISER THAT HE,
"YET, YOU, AGROWN MAN, DID NOT WISELY CONSULT ME."

"CHRISTIAN DO YOU NOT KNOW, CAN YOU NOT SEE?
YOU ARE MY SHILD, YES I AM A "HOLY FATHER" TO THEE!

"MORESO THAN THE CHILD ASKING WHAT TO DO, WHAT TO BE;
WITH YOUR EVERY DECISION YOU SHOLD CONSULT WITH ME."

"Through a Childs Eyes"

LIFE SOMETIMES STRANGE AND COMPLICATED SEEMS

THROUGH HUMAN EYES AND DREAMS.

YOU CAN LOOK AROUND AND WONDER JUST

WHY; SOME ARE BLESSED FROM THE SKY.

SOME HAVE SO MUCH; WEALTH PLUS INHERITANCE

AND ALL THAT THEY WISH FOR:

YET WHEN LOOKING AROUND THEM THEY

SEE THAT SOME ARE HAPPIER POOR!

I HAVE A LARGE FAMILY TO CARE FOR; YET CRAVE MORE WRITING TIME:

FORGETTING TO BE THANKFUL FOR BLESSINGS

I RECEIVE; TIME AFTER TIME!

BUT GOD SEES WITH A LOVING AND KIND EYE,

THOUGH AT TIMES I ASK; "WHY?"

HE KNOWS, WITHOUT FAMILY TO CARE FOR I'D WASTE MY LIFE; AND CRY!

HE KNOWS THAT I LOOK THROUGH DULL HUMAN

EYES, AND WILL SOON REALIZE

THROUGH MY HUMAN EYES I CAN NEVER SEE PURE TRUTHS A CHILD SEES!

I RECALL: BECAUSE OF MANS' SIN THE HUMAN

EYE IS CLOUDED, HALF BLIND!

BUT THROUGH THE INNOCENT CHILDS EYES SO

BRIGHT; THE PURE TRUTH YOU CAN FIND!

A SMALL CHILD IS INNOCENT, CAN SEE TRUTH:

THROUGH DEDICATION, LOVE.

AS GOD'S CHILD WE CAN ASK FOR ENLIGHTMENT

FROM THE SAVIOR ABOVE!

"To a Friend"

WE'RE MUCH TOO ALIKE TO DISAGREE;

OR DO YOU DISAGREE WITRH ME?

WE HAVE TOO MUCH IN COMMON TO DEBATE,

OR DID YOU FIND WE DIFFER AS OF LATE?

YES, THERE IS A COMMON BOND BETWEEEN

YOU AND I, AS IF IT WERE QUEEN TO QUEEN.

NO MATTER HOW DIFERENT OUR LIVES MAY BE

WE'VE FELT THE LOAD OF THE WORLD, YOU…ME.

WE'VE LEARNED FROM DOING, AND LEARNED FROM GOD

THAT BENEATH OUR TOIL OUR HEADS WILL NOD.

YET SOMEHOW WE CANNOT REST, BUT CARRY ON

'TILL WHATEVER LOAD WE CARRY, ITS' TOIL IS DONE.

WE BOTH KNOW HOW TODO WHAT MUST BE DONE,

NO MATTER HOW IT TEARS DOWN TO THE VERY BONE.

LIVING IS HARD AS WE'VE BOTH COME TO KNOW.

WITH THIS KNOWLEDGE IN COMMON, MAY OUR FRIENDSHIP GROW!

"To Be Free"

OH THAT MY HEART, MY SOUL, MY BEING WERE FREE

TO READ, TO WRITE, TO PONDER, TO LOVE, TO BE ME!

OH PHILOSOPHY: WITH YOU MY HERT IS ENTWINED:

BUT NEVER FREE TO LIVE, TO INDULGE; DRINK AND DINE!

OH WERE I NOT TIED TO DAILY CHORES AND BORES

BUT COULD I ROAM O'ER LAND AND O'ER THE SHORES!

OH WERE I FREE TO READ, WRITE, THINK, LOVE; TO BE:

JUST TO DREAM AND LIVE IN DREAMS IRRESPONSIBLY!

OH TO TRAVEL BACK IN TIME WITH BARDS AND SEARCH

PAST, PRESENT, FURTURE, AND FIND MY LIFES WORTH!

OH FOR WHAT LIVE I? FOR I CAN NE'ER ANSWER CALL

TO WHAT MEANS SO MUCH TO ME; COULD TO ALL!

OH TO SEARCH THE KNOWLEDE OF BARDS WORLD O'ER

AND CONTRIBUTE MY THOUGHTS TO PAGE FOREVER MORE!

OH LIFE ESCAPE ME NOT TILL MY LIFE BECOMES FREE

TO SEARCH, TO LIVE, TO WRITE; CONTRIBUTE MY PHILOSPHY!

IT SEEMS I WAS A LITTLE IMPATIENT. MUCH OLDER

NOW I HAVE AMPLE TIME FOR POETRY!

I THANK THE LORD FOR GIVNG ME THIS OPORTUNITY!

"To Charlie"
(TRUEST OF IRISH HEARTS)

AH, THERE WAS BRAVEHEART; SCOTTISH THROUGH AND THROUGH
THE BEST OF THE FIGHTING IRISH FOUGHT FOR HIM TRUE!

THERE WAS LIONHEART; POWER, BENEATH COOL!
ON A DAILY BASIS WE SEE THE SAME POWER IN YOU!

NEXT; THERE WAS TRUEHEART; WITH LOVE EVER TRUE'
YOU LOVE! WHATEVER BEFALLS NEVER CHANGES YOU!

THEN THERE IS THE GIVING HEART, GIVING THROUGH IT ALL.
YOU GIVE AND GIVE; YOU WILL BE GIVING 'TILL YOU FALL!

HIDDEN; IS THE CHERISHING HEART, TREASURING EACH;
AS YOU PONDER EACH ONE: JOY MEASURES COMPLETE!

LAST; THERE IS THE SERVING HEART; LOVES' TEST TRUE!
WE ALL KNOW DEAR HEART, WE CAN DEPEND ON YOU!

TO MY DEAR BROTHER-IN-LAW: CHARLES BARNES.

"To Emma When Sick"

A RAINBOW AND UNICORN

TO MAKE SWEET CHEEKS GLOW

AND A "SWEET WARM HEART.

COMFORT YOUR SOUL!

GET WELL EMMA LOU!

AND BACK HOME.

WE ALL MISS YOU

WHEN YOU'RE GONE!

MAY ANGELS 'NEATH YOUR PILLOW

AND OUR FATHERS' LOVE

HELP MAKE YOU WELL NOW

WITH STRENGTH FROM ABOVE!

"To Lead Others to Thee"

TODAY I'LL WASH MY OLD SELF ALL AWAY;
THEN GO DOWN TO BETHEL TO PRAY.
THANK YOU LORD FOR SAVING MY SOUL,
THANK YOU LORD FOR GUIDING ME SO.

THANK YOU FOR BLESSINGS I BARELY CONTAIN!
THANK YOU LORD, YOU BROUGHT ME CLOSE AGAIN!
SHOW ME HOW I CAN SERVE YOU BEST;
LEAD OTHERS TO LEAN ON THY BREAST.

LORD I FEEL AS BLESSED AS THY BELOVED JOHN
MY GOAL IS TO SERVE THE AS HE HAS DONE!
I FEEL DEAR LORD, SOON YOU WILL COME.
LEAD ME LORD TO EACH CHOSEN ONE!

"To: Little Effie May"

LITTLE PRETTY PETITE EFFY MAY

HER SMILE BRIGHTENS OUR WORK DAY!

SHE WORKS HARD WHEN I NEED HER TOO

THEN SHE SITS WITH COFFEE TOO!

LIVELY AS PURE HOT PEPPERMINT,

BUT SO SWEEET, SHE'S HEAVEN SENT!

WE COULD NOT DO WITRHOUT HER,

WITH HER SMILE AND CUSTOMER CHATTER!

SHE WORKS EFFORTLESSLY ON THE HARDEST JOB

THEN SITS LAZILY AWHILE LIKE SHE'S TIRED!

THOUGH HER BOSS, I INVITE HER TO SIT WITH ME,

HAVE A BIT OF TALK AND COFFEE.

SHE IS EVER READY TO LAUGH OUT LOUD.

THHEN AT TIMES SHE'S BASAHFUL AND PROUD.

SHE SEEMSYOUNG AS YOUNG CAN BE

YET SHE IS THE MOTHER OF THREE!

I LOVE HER LITTLE MISCHIEVIOS SMILE.

TO COME WHEEN NEEDED SHE'S WALK A MILE;

TO COMEWHEN SHE IS NEEDED HERE!

BUT MOST OF ALL WE NEED HER CHEER!

"To My Mother"

WHEN I LOST MY LOVE,

SHE TOLD ME HER LOVE STORY;

LIFE, IN ALL ITS' GLORY,

STOOD BEFORE ME AND ABOVE!

MY MOTHER'S GETTING OLD; HER BODY IS WORN.

I CANNOT GIVE HER MY STORY, POETRY, SONG.

NOR CAN I RETURN HER LOST YEARS, FOREVER GONE.

I CANNOT SHORTEN THE YEARS SINCE I WAS BORN, STILL:

WHILE MOTHERS' HAIR IS GRAY;

WRINKLED IS HER SOFT FACE:

ANGELS WILL RESTORE HER GRACE,

SOFTLY: SONG, POETRY, LIFE WILL FLOAT AWAY!

"To Thy Crystal Waters, Lead On"

I'M ANXIOUS TO TRAVEL LEAD ON!

THOUGH THE JOURNENY BE ROUGH I'LL GO

PLEASE LEAD ME NOW, LORD LEAD ME ON:

TO WHERE THY CRYSTAL WATERS FLOW!

WHEN I GET THERE, I'LL BE WEARY:

I SHALL COOL MY DUST TRODDEN FEET;

RINSE WAY CARES OF THE JOURNEY,

THEN, OTHER TRAVELERS I'LL MEET!

THE PATH MAY ET DUSTY AND DRY

BENEATH THE HOT AND SCORCHING SUN.

WE'LL REACH COOL WATER BYE AND BYE

TO SOAK CONTENTED, VICT-RY WON!

I KNOW LORD, THE WAY IS HARD AND STEEP

BUT I'LL FOLLOW, THROUGH THE LAST MILE:

TRY NOT TARRY, LONG THE WAY; KEEP

ON THY PATH, DO MY BEST, AND SMILE!

FRIENDS TO FOLLOW 'LONG, ON THY PATH.

WE CAN RINSE OFF THE DUST AND CLAY

IN JORDANS' COOL, SWEET CRYSTAL BATH!

HELP ME NOW LORD, AS I MEET FRIENDS,

TELL HOW YOU WASH THEM, WHITE AS SNOW.

SHOW THEM THY PATH, HOW TO BEGIN;

AND BRING OTHER, THAT WISW TO GO!

REACHING JORDAN, SO SWEET, SO DEAR:

ONE BY ONE; FEET HEAVY AND RED:

HE'LL WASH OUR PAIN, OUR HEARTACHES, CLEAR

VICT-RY WON, WORK DONE, NEVER DEAD!

"Watch Nature"

WATCH THE BLUEJAY SAILING THROUGH THE AIR.

WATCH THE FLIGHT OF THE GREAT HAWK.

WATCH SPARROWS FLITTING AWAY. WATCH THE

HUMMINGBIRD STAND STILL IN MID AIR!

WATCH THE WIND BLOW THROUGH THE TREES.

WATCH THE WAVES WASH UP ON THE BEACH.

WATCH THE SOFT BREEZE BLOWING THROUGH THE

GRASS. WATCH THE WATER BUBBLE UP OVER THE

ROCKS. WATCH THE SLEEPING BABY SWEETLY SMILE.

WATCH THE LITTLE CHILD AS SHE PLAYS.

WATCH THE LOVE OF THE BRAND NEW MOTHER.

WATCH THE FLUSH OF THE YOUG GIRLS FACE!

WATCH THE BEAUTY OF A BRAND NEW BRIDE. WATCH

THE LOVE IN THAT BOY AND GIRLS EYES!

WATCH THE PRIDE FOR A DEED OF A YOUNG BOY. WATCH

THE LITLLE GIRL AS SHE GETS A NEW DRESS.

WATCH THE HORSES RACE ACROSS THE FIELD. WATCH

THE SQUIRREL RUN UP INTO THE TREE.

WATCH THE NEW BORN CALF TAKE ITS MILK.

WATCH THE DEER AS THEY SWIFTLY RUN!

GOD THEIR CREATER MADE THEM ALL WITH GREAT LOVE!

"Wava Carol Rhorer Griffis"

OUR "FATHEER" CREATED IN HER
A VERY RARE SWEET BOUQUET:
A WAVE OF COUNTRY ELEGANCE
WITH AN AURA BRIGHT AND GAY!

HER BEAUTIFUL SWEET BOUGUET:
"A SPECIAL FRAGRANCE OF HER LOVE;"
WAFTED THE LIVES SHE LOVED,
LIKE WHISPERING WINGS OF A DOVE!

"We Are All Children"

CHILDREN LEARN BY SLOW TRIAL AND ERROR. THE
BABE LETS GO, TAKES A STEP AND FALLS:
YET TRIES AGAIN, DESPITE THE FEARS; FROM A
"DRIVE TO STRIVE" INBORN IN US ALL!
ALSO THEY LEARN BY MANY GUIDING HANDS OF
PARENTS TEACHERS, PEERS AND SUCH,
UNTIL THEY ADAPT, JUST AS PLANNED: GROWN
TO WOMAN OR MAN KNOWING MUCH!

YET SURPRISINGLY I HAVE FOUND OUT ADULTS
MUST LEARN TOO, EACH NEW DAY
BY TRIAL AND ERROE, WITHOUT DOUBT; HIGH
THE COST OF ERRORS, THEY CAN PAY!

GUIDING THE INNOCENT TINY TOTS FAILURE
OR SUCCESS WE TEACH THEM.
PONDER WHAT TO DO AND WHAT NOT…THEY
ARE GODS' CREATION, LIFE AND LIMB!
AS ADULTS WE ARE GUIDES AND TEACHERS,
THOUGH WE MAKE ERRORS, EVEN NOW.
WE MUST, THROUGH GODS' WORD, BE SEEKERS:
FOR HE ALONE CAN NOT, DOES NOT FAIL!

GOD LEADS US, AS WE LEAD THE SWEET BABE.
HE GUIDES US, AS WE GUIDE A CHILD.
WE'RE HIS CHILDREN FROM BIRTH TO GRAVE:
TILL WE JOIN HIM, AT THE END OF LIFES' TRIALS!

"We Are So Few"

OUR PASTOR PREACHED A WAY OF FORGIVENESS
FOR EAACH BRETHRENS ERRORS AND SINS.
HIS SERMON PAINTED A BEAUTIFUR PORTRAIT
SHOWING SALVATION FOR ALL; DEAR OR KIN.

AND TEARS FLOWED TO MY EYE
AS THE BRETHREN SO FEW SAT THERE.
FIR JUST A SMASLL HANDFUL WERE WE,
AND SO MANY NEED GODS' CARE!

WHAT MUST WE DO LITTLE HANDFUL OF MEN?
GODS' WORDS ARE TAUGHT EACH SERVICE ANEW.
THEY CANNOT BE IN VAIN, BRING PEOPLE I N!
UPON FAITHE WE MUST BUILD AND FILL EACH PEW!

PRAY FOR INCREASE IN THE LORDS' CREW.
COME TO ALL SERVICES, GOD NEEDS YOU!
WHEN YOU COME, INVITE A FRIEND,
AND WORK TO BRING OUR FAMILY ALL IN!

"We Have a Son"

OUR SINFUL EARTH LOOKS DARK
MAKING BEAUTY HARD TO SEE
HIDDEN IN SHADOWS FROM OUR HEARTS
AS SO DISTRACTED ARE WE.

WORSE THE WORLD WILL BECOME
THEN OUR LORDS' GIFT OF BEAUTY
WE'LL SEE MUCH LESS IN TIMES TO COME
OUR ONLY HOPE IS GODS' SON!

WE HAVE JESUS, GOD'S SON
TO FOLLOW; A LIFE APART!
WHEN THESE SINFUL TIMES ARE DONE
IN DARKNESS, WE HAVE A "SON"!

"Welcome Friend"

I'M SO GLAD YOU CALLED AND YOU'RE COMING BY!
IT MAKES ME FEEL LIKE TELLING YOU JUST WHY!

FRIEND YOU KNOW YOU ARE JUST THE APPLE OF MY EYE
AND THER CLOSEST FRIEND I HAVE ON EARTH, 'NEATH THE SKY!

NO ONE ELSE COULD BE SO WELCOME WHEN I'M WEARY AND DREAR
AS YOU DO, GOOD FRIEND, I CHERISH SO VERY DEAR!

I'M TIRED AND WEARY, WORKING WITH STRANGERS, I NEED CHEER!
SO I'M SO VERY PLEASED TO HEAR YOU SAY YOU'RE COMING HERE!
TO EDITH

"What is Our Destiny?"

HE SMILED AND SAID HE LOVED ME,

MY HEART LEAPT UP WITH PRIDE.

HE SAID THAT HE HATED THE GROUND I WEALKED ON,

MY HEART WAS BROKEN BUT I SURVIVED!

HEY, HO, WHAT ARE PEOPLE GOING TO DO?

HEY, HA, DOES ANYONE KNOW WHERE THEY ARE?

NO ONE KNOWS THERE FEELINGS ANYMORE:

FIGHT AND FUSS SND CURSE; NOT KNOWING WHAT FOR!

ONCE I THOUGHT I LOVED A BOY IN TENNESSEE,

NEXT I KNEW I WISHED FOR ANOTHERS ARMS!

THE BOY IN TENNESSEE WAS AWFULLY FAR AWAY

AND THE ONE OIIN MY TOWN HAD MANY CHARMS!

IT SEEMS YOU LOVE THE ONE WHO'S IN SIGHT,

TEMPATION IS GREATER SOMEHOW THAN EVER;

EVERYONE LOVES ONE UNTIL THEY MEET ANOTHER!

TELL ME PEOPLE, WHAT IS OUR DESTINATION?

AND WHATEVER ARE OUR CHILDREN GOING TO DO?

WILL THEY HAVE REAL LOVE AND UNDERSTANDING?

WE DON'T EVEN UNDERSTAND ME OR YOU?

"Who Else Lord"

WHO ELSE CAN BURN POTATOES LORD
WIRTHOUT LEAVING THE KITCHEN EVEN ONE TIME?
'TWOULD BE SUCH A BLESSING IF FOR
THE TIMES I GOOFED MEALS I HAD A DIME!

BUT YOUR BLESSINGS ARE SENT OFTEN ENOUGH
MORE THAN I DESERVE, AND THAT'S A FACT.
STILL, THE DAYS BRIGHTER WITH YOUR TOUCH
AND I ASK AGAIN; "PLEASE KEEP ME IN TACT?"

YOU KNOW THE GOOD THOUGHTS IN MY HEART
AND OH HOW OFT YOU FORGIVE THE BAD.
JUST HELP ME "THE GOOD TO OTHERS GIVE A PART
AND TEACH ME TO SUPPRESS THE "EVIL" AND THE "SAD".

LET ME, DEAREST LORD, BRING CHEER TO OTHERS LIVES.
TO MAKE IMPORTANT ALL MY LITTLE FAILURES
AND PASS THE JOY ON TO OTHER BUSY WIVES;
LORD YOU ARE THE "UPPER WE NEED IN THIS DAY OF OURS!

"Yellow Curtains"

GIVE ME A HME IN THE COUNTRY WHERE
THE WEEPING WILLOWS MOURN.
HERE THE TINY WILD FLOWERS PEEP OUT SO EARLY IN THE SPRING.
THE BIRDS SING IN THE TREES AND CROWS
CAW O'ER THE FIELD OF CORN.

GIVE ME A JOME IN THE COUNTRY, TUCKED BENEATH THE TREES,
YELLOW CURTAINS IN THER KITCHEN SWAYED BY S SUMMER BREEZE.
VEGETABLES FROM THE GARDEN, GATHERED IN EARLY MORN,
FRESH MILK, COUNTRY BUTTER, AND GOLDEN YELLOW CORN.

WHERE THE TINY WHITE FLOWERS PEEP OUT ON THEIR VERY OWN
MAKING YOU FEEL LIKE A YOUNG CHILD BACK HOME.
WHERE THE BIRDS SEEM TI GATHER TO MAKE A HUGE ORCHESTRA
THAT WAKENS ME EACH MORNING; TO A BRIGHT SUMMER DAY!

GIVE ME A HOME IN THE COUNTRY TUCKED BENEATH THE TREES,
AWAY FROM THE CITY WHERE LIFE IS LIKE A HUGE HIVE OF BEES.
WITH YELLOW CURTAINS IN THE KITCHEN SWAYED AY A SUMMER BREEZE.

"You Speak Falsely Leigh"

YOU SPEAK FALSELY OF WANTING TO DIE MY DEAR CHILD!

YOUR EYES ARE YET PRETTY, SO ALIVE AND WILD.

WHEN YOU'VE GIVEN UP THE WILL TO LIVE MY DEAR,

ONES EYES TURN DULL AND EMPTY, LOOK TO NOWHERE.

EYES OF ONE WHO IS TRULY READY FOR DEATH

HAVE NO SUCH SPARKLE; HAVE NO DEPTH.

YOUSR EYES MAY NOT SPARKLE CONSTANTLY, TRUE,

BUT AT YOUR SADDEST, A POOL OF DEPTH SHINES THROUGH!

IT TAKES ONLY A NOTION TO BRING A SPARKLE THERE;

AND NOT MUCH MORE TO LIGHT THE DEEP GREEN FIRE!

YES, YOU SPEAK FALSELY OF WANTING TO DIE MY LEIGH,

THERE'S TOO MUCH LIFE IN YOUR EYES TO SEE.

'TIS ONLY A WHIM THAT YOU HAVE SWEEET LASS

AND AS QUICKLY AS ITCAME IT SHALL PASS.

'TIS ONLY VIVID IMAGINATIION DRIVING YOU I DEEM

THERES'S TOO MUCH LIFE AND SPRARKLE IN YOUR EYES SO GREEN!

"Your Unborn Babe"

FRIEND O F MINE WITH SUCH TENDER HEART
DO NOT CRY FOR THE LOSS OF YOUR UNBORN BABE.
IT DID NOT KNOW THE JOY OF LIFE FROM WHICH IT DID DEPART;
NOR OF SADDNESS, OR TEARS, LIFE WOULD HAVE GAVE.

YOU PICTURED THE BABY AT YOUR LOVING BREAST
YET IT KNEW NOT OF SUCH A TENDER COZY NEST. IT DID NOT!
IT DID NOT KNOW AND SHALL NEVER MISS
LIFE, YOUR LOVE OR YOUR MOTHERLY TENDERNESS,

DO NOT BROOD O'ER THE ONE WHO HAS GONE
YOU HAVE OTHERTS NOW TO NURSE 'TILL GROWN.
YOUR HEART, FOR THE "ONE LOST" WILL LONG.
THEN CHECK TO SEE THE OTHERS; HAPPINESS KNOW!

"Youth"

IN TAKING A LOOK AT THE CITY ALL AROUND;
MEMORIES AND YOUTH I SAW.....RE-FOUND!
AS USUAL THERE WERE PEOPLE AT CROSSOADS;
BIG, SMALL, RICH AND POOR, ALL CODES.

AT AN INTERSECTION I SAW A GIRL IN HER TEENS
SHOUTING TO OTHERS NEAR-BY; SOMETHING OBSCENE.
MY MEMORY SWEPT BACK TO MY IMPERTINENT YOUTH,
AND TO THE CHIDING LAUGHTER OF THE SAME.

REMEMBERING HOW I FELT THEN, OF THE WORLD IN MY YOUTH
I REALIZED ANEW THAT THEY ARE NOT REALLY TO BLAME!
A TEENAGER WILL FOLLOW HIS PEERS TO A CERTAIN EXTENT;
AND TO OTHERS IMMORAL IDEAS AND PLNS, THEY ARE BENT.

BUT HOW FAR THEY GO DEPENDS QUITE A LOT
UPON WHAT THEY ARE TAUGHT AND WHAT THEY'RE NOT!
THEN THEIR CONSCIENCE; IF GOD THERE ABIDES;
WILL KEEP THEM FROM TOO FAR WRONG, TO SLIDE!

PROSE; LONG POEMS;
STORY POEMS

"A Desperate Prayer"

OH JUMBLED MASS OF TROUBLE IN MY MIND
WHERE AND WHEN, FROM YOU, PECE WILL I FIND?
MUST ONE FOREVER, WHILE HERE ON EARTH
STRUGGLE THROUGH SUCH MESSED UP MIRTH?

IF SO, I LOOK FORWARD TOWARDS THE END;
ON HIGHER GROUND THIS MESS I KNOW WILL END!
AT TIMES I FEEL UPON ME IS A CURSE
THAT HAS BEEN THERE SINCE MY BIRTH.

IF SO, MY LORD; TAKE THIS CURSE AWAY,
IT GROWS TOO HEAVY FOR ME TODAY.
SOON ITS' WEIGHT WILL CRUSH MY BODY BELOW.
MY PURPOSE HERE I SHALL NEVER TRULY KNOW!

TAKE THIS JUMBLED TROUBLE AWAY FROM ME
SO MY MIND CAN WORK WHEN SET FREE.
HELP ME TO DO WHAT I WAS PUT HERE FOR,
SHOW MEMY LORD, THE CORRECT DOOR!

"A Pastor With a Pure Heart"

PASTOR DEWAYNE WALKER LOVES THE LORD WITH ALL HIS HEART.

HE GIVES HIS ALL. AT CHURCH EARLY EVERY MORN

HE PRAYS FOR THE FLOCK, AND ALL THOSE UPON HIS HEART.

KNOCKING ON DOORS WITH HIS BIBLE, A PATHWAY HE'S WORN.

MINUTES AFTER HE MEETS A STRANGER BOLDLY HE'LL ASK;

"IF YOU DIED TONIGHT DO YOU KNOW YOU'D GO TO HEAVEN?"

SHARING THE LORD'S GOSPEL DAILY IS HIS MAIN TASK

HIS CHURCH RUNS A CHILDREN'S BUS MINISTREY: BRINGS THEM IN!

HE WALKS WITH GREAT GUSTO AND HAS THE MOST WINNING SMILE;

VISITS THE SICK, SPEAKS AT FUNERALS AND WEDDINGS.

THEN ON RADIO HE SPREADS THE GOSPEL FOR MILES!

HE NEVER SEEMS TO STOP; FOR THE LORD HE DOES ALL THINGS!

HE PREACHES THE OLD ST. JAMES BIBLE; BELIEVES THE WORDS:

THAT THEY CAME FROM GOD, EVERY WORD FROM GOD'S HEART!

HE LOVES THE LORD, HIS FAMILY, AND HE LOVES YOU!

HIS WORK AND DETERMINATION COME FROM A TRUE, PURE HEART!

THEY RUN BUSSES TO PICK UP CHILDREN; MANY HAVE NEEDS!

THESE CHILDREN ARE LOVED AND TAUGHT THAT JESUS LOVES THEM.

HIS WIFE SANDY WORKS CONSTANTLY FILLING ALL NEEDS:

FOR THE CHURCH, FOR WOMEN ACTIVITIES; AND BESIDE HIM.

I'VE ATTENDED CHURCHES IN SEVERAL STATES AND HERE

IN KENTUCKY. NO OTHER COMPARES TO THE HEART

THAT'S FOUND IN MOUNT OLIVETS' SWEET CHURCH ATMOSPHERE;

AND FOUND IN HARD WORKING PASTOR DEWANE WALKERS PURE HEART!

Bible School: Year 1955

CHILDREN'S PASTOR: PASTOR CLARENCE WALKER

BACK IN THE DAY, FOLKS SHARED, MOST PRAYED.
A CHURCH IN TOWN HELD BIBLE SCHOOL
AND WELCOMED SMALLER CHURCHES TO JOIN IN.
MANY SMALL CHURCHES COULD NOT
FINANCE THEIR OWN BIBLE SCHOOL. OUR NEIGHBORS
CHURCH WAS INVITED. SHE WAS MRS. CHIPLEY.
SHE INVITED ME TO GO TO THE BIBLE SCHOOL IN
TOWN. I SAID I WOULD GO DESPITE BEING
BACKWARD AND SHY! MY YOUNGER BROTHER
DECIDED TO GO TOO. A BIG BLUE BUS
WAS TAKING US AND HE KNEW IT WOULD BE FUN.
WE WENT TO CLASS, MUCH LIKE A SUNDAY SCHOOL
CLASS. THEN WE WENT TO THE LARGE
AUDITORIUM. SHOES SCUFFLED ON THE WOOD FLOOR
AS WE SHUFFLED AROUND TO FIND A GOOD
SEAT. THE AUDITORIUM WAS FULL! EVERYONE WAS
EXCITED AND WHISPERING THAT PASTOR WALKER
WAS COMING.
FINALLY, A TALL COUNTRY LOOKING FELLOW WALKED
ON STAGE, CAME TO THE CENTER; THEN
WALKED UP TO THE VERY EDGE. HE LEANED FORWARD
A BIT, LOOKED DOWN AND FROM ONE SIDE TO
THE OTHER AT ALL OF US. THEN HE SMILED! HIIS SMILE
WENT FROM EAR TO EAR! INSTANTLY YOU FELT

HE WAS YOUR FRIEND! AND HE WAS! PASTOR CLARENCE

WALKERS' HAIR WAS WIND BLOWN, HIS

JACKET A LITTLE SNUG AND HIS SHOES WORN. HE JUST

LOOKED COUNTRY: BUTY HE HAD A BRILLANT

"MASTER PLAN." HE WAS DETERMINED TO TEACH (EACH

OF US ABLE TO UNDERSTAND) THE MEANING

OF SALVATION: JUST IN ONE WEEK!

HE LED US IN SINGING "JESUS LOVES THE LITTLE

CHILDREN." HE ASKED US TO HOLD OUR BIBLES

WAY UP HIGH AND EXPLAINED THAT WORDS IN THE

BIBLE WERE OUR ARMOUR TO FIGHT AGAINST

SATAN. WE STOOD; SANG AND MARCHED TO "ONWARD

CHRISTIAN SOLDIERS." PASTOR WALKER

MARCHED WITH US. THEN WE SANG "ONE, TWO, THREE

THE DEVILS AFTER ME." "FOUR, FIVE, SIX

HE'S ALWAYS THROWING BRICKS." "SEVEN, EIGHT, NINE

HE MISSES ALL THE TIME." HALLELUJAH, I'M

SAVED.

SO FAR PASTOR WALKER HAD TAUGHT US; AFTER EACH

SONG; JESUS LOVED US, WE COULD STAND

UP FOR JESUS WITH HIS WORD, AND HE HELPED FIGHT

FOR THE SAVED. WE SANG 'THIS LITTLE LIGHT OF

MINE' AND 'I'LL BE A SUNBEAM FOR JESUS.' WE WERE ALL

WANTING TO LET OUR LITTLE LIGHTS SHINE

FOR THIS MAN, GODS' SON WHO DIED TO SAVE US FROM

SIN AND SATAN! HE EXPLAINED TO US: FROM

HIS BIG HEART; THAT JESUS CAME AND KNOCKED ON

YOUR HEARTS DOOR. ONES OLD ENOUGH ALL

UNDERSTOOD THIS WITH NO PROBLEM. PASTOR WALKER
TOLD US HOW WE COULD ACCEPT OR REJECT
JESUS. HE EXPLAINED HOW YOU NEEDED TO PROFESS
TO ACCEPT JESUS AS YOUR SVIOUR! HE TOLD US
THE REASON FOR BAPTISM. HE EXPLAINED WHAT AN
INVITATION WAS; THEN WE SANG "JUST AS I AM."
AS WE SANG "JUST AS I AM;" THE WORDS BRTOUGHT
TEARS TO MY EYES. JESUS WANTED ME,
EVEN ME, TO BE A CHILD OF GOD! I FOUND MYSELF
STANDING; BASHFUL OR NOT, AND I WALKED
DOWN THAT AISLE I ASKED JESUYS INTO MY HEART.
I GLANCED AT THE OTHER SIDE OF THE
AUDITORIUM AND SAW MY BROTHER WALKING DOWN
TOO! I WAS SO HAPPY! IT WAS HARD TALKING
THROUGH TEARS, TELLING THE LADY AT THE
ALTER I WAS SAVED. SHE UNDERSTOOD.
I WANT TO EVER BE A SUNBEAM FOR JESUS! HE CHANGED
MY LIFE FROM EMPTY TO FULL. HE WAS
WITH ME THROUGH TROUBLES I COULD NOT
HAVE COME THROUGH WITH OUT HIM!
IF JESUS KNOCKS ON YOUR DOOR
I HOPE YOU WILL LET HM IN!
OPEN UP YOUR HEARTS DOOR:
WE'LL ALL MEET IN HEAVEN!

"Dearest Lord Jesus"

I HUMBLY COME, BURDENED SORELY FOR MY CHILDREN
AND GRANDCHILDREN. I GIVE THANKS AND

PRAISE FOR YOUR MANY, MANY BLESSSINGS; FOR
FORGIVENESS WHEN I ERR; FOR BEAUTY ALL

AROUND IN NATURE, GIVEN SO GRACIOPUSLY; FOR
YOUR PROMISE THAT THE CIRCLE WILLL BE

UNBROKEN; FOR THE HOPE OF HEAVENS SHORES; FOR
YOUR POWER TO HEAL THE HEART AND SOUL;

FOR YOUR COMFORT GIVEN IN TIME OF NEED; FOR
YOUR WATCH-KEEP OVER ALL YOUR OWN; FOR

MIRACLES AND VISIONS, SHOWN TO ME THROUGHT
MY LIFE; FOR HOPE YOU PUT IN MY HEART AS A

SMALL CHILD; FOR LOVE YOU PUT IN MY HEART; FOR
ALL GOOD IN ME; I THANK YOU FOR ALL YOUR
GIFTS; I PRAISE YOU!
LEAD ME THIS DAY LORD. LEAD ME TO GUIDE MY
FAMILY IN THIS TROUBLED DAY. SOME OF THEM

ARE SORELY TROUBLES, THE WORLD IS A CRUEL PLACE
IN THIS DAY. ILLNESS INHERITED, PLAGUES US.

SATAN IS AGAINST US IN EVERY WAY. LORD TELL ME
WHAT TO DO. MY HEART CRIES. MY HEART

ACHES. MY ONLY STRENGTH IS IN THEE. MY ONLY
HOPE IS IN THEE. THOU ART GREAT LORD!

THOUPART ALL POWERFUL! HELP THIS FAMILY LORD.
SEND ANGELS TO PROTECT US. SEND THEM TO

BATTELE FOR US AGAINST ALL SATANS' EVIL TRICKS.
HAVE MERCY UPON MY CHILDREN OH LORD.

HAVE MERCY AND FORGIVENESS. CALL THEIR HEARTS
BACK TO THEE LORD. RE-AWAKEN THE LOVE,

THE GOODNESS AND HOPE WITHIN THEM. GIVE THEM
KNOWLEDGE OF EVIL FILTERED INTO THEIR

LIVES. COME TO COMBAT FOR THEM. OH MY BLESSED
SAVIOR. HAVE MERCY UPON MY LITTLE BABIES.

REMEMBER LORD, THE DAY THEY GAVE THEIR HEARTS
TO YOU. THE DAY THEIR NAMES WERE

WRITTEN IN YOUR BOOK. THE DAY THE ANGELS SANG
AND REJOICED. OH BLESSED LORD, REMEMBER

THE SWEET FRAGRANCE OF LOVE FROM THEIR HEARTS,
AND FROM MINE. REMEMBER OH LORD AND

HAVE PITY UPON THEM IN THEIR FALLEN STATE. REMOVE EVIL
INFLUENCE FROM THEM. OPEN THEIR EYES AND HEARTS OH LORD.
THANK YOU LORD FOR BEING MY HOPE, MY LIGHT.
DIRECT ME IN THY WAYS THAT I SHOULD PLEASE

THEE. HELP ME WITH MY WORK NOW FOR THEE. LORD
MAY I SEE THE DAY WHEN TALENTS OF MY

CHILDREN AND GRANDCHILDREN ARE USED FOR THY
GLORY LORD, I PRAY FOR THAT DAY. THANK YOU

H LORD OF LORDS, OH TRUTH THAT IS. POWER PASSING
ALL OTHER POWERS, LOVE SURPASSING ALL

LOVE, GIVER OF BEAUTY SURPASSING ALL BEAUTIFUL.
I LOVE THEE OH MY LORD. I PRAISE THEE. I

HOPE IN THEE. I CHOOSE TO FOLLOW THY WAYS. GUIDE
ME IN THY WAYS. THANK YOU OH MY GREAT

AND GRACIOUS LORD. IT IS THEE AND THEE ALONE
THAT HAS MADE LIVING AND WORKING

WORTHWHILE. YOU THAT HAS BEEN THERE WHEN
NEEDED, THAT HAS GIVEN SO BOUNTIFULLY TO

ONE SO POOR. THANK YOU OH LORD, THANK YOU FOR
ALL I HAVE THAT IS GOOD, THAT COMETH

FROM THEE. THANK YOU FOR ALL HELP I HAVE HAD
IN MY YEARS. GUIDE ME LORD, I KNOW NOT

WHAT TO DO. GUIDE MY FAMILY. THANK YOU LORD
FOR BEING ALWAYS THERE, ALWAYS COMING

THROUGH WHEN NEEDED. THE ONLY HELP FOR
THE TROUBLED. AMEN, AND AMEN!

"God Son"

WHEN YOU WERE A TINY BABY I WEATCHED AS YOU WULD SLEEP.

YOU SMILED AT ALL THE ANGELS, OH SO ADORABLE AND SWEET.

I KNOW 'TWAS ANGELS YOU SMILED AT, FOR YOUR CHEEKS DID GLOW;

AND IT IS SO BAD JEFF, HOW MUCH LESS WE SEE ANGELS AS WE GROW.

BUT THEY WATCHED OVER YOU, SO TINY AS YOU SLEPT,

AND YOU SAFETY AND CONTENTMENT THEY GUARDED AND KEPT!

THEN AS YOU BECAME A TODDLER. THEY PROTECTED YOU II KNOW,

FOR WE'TRE EACH GIVEN A GUARDIAN ANGEL, THE SCRIPTURES SAY SO!

NOW JEFFERY, YOU'RE TOO BIG FOR A GUARDIAN ANGEL,

BUT DON'T FORGET THEY WERE THERE, AND JESUS BY YOUR SIDE STILL.

DO GOOD TO OTHERS, THE YOUNG AND ELDERLY WHO BEFRIENDED YOU,

THE STRANGER AND THE NEEDY? BEKIND. DO THE GOOD YOU CAN DO.

WITHOUT THE ANGELS GUIDING HAND YOU ARE RESPONSIBLE NOW;

THEY PROTECTED YOU BEFORE; NOW YOU'RE ON YOUR OWN PAL!

THE CHOICE IS YOURS FROM NOW ON TO DO GOOD OR BAD.

JESUS STANDS THERE LOVINGLY WAITING FOR

YOU TO MAKE HIM SAD OR GLAD!

I'M GLAD YOU MADE YOUR DECISION TO LIVE FOR CHRIST THAT DAY,

BUT YOU MUST KEEP ON CHOOSING IN MANY DIFFERENT WAYS.

THERE IS ALLWAYS A DECISION, CHOOSE CHRIST TO GUIDE EACH CHOICE,

FOR NO LONGER IS YOUR ANGEL PUSHING AWAY EACH STONE!

THIS MAY ALL SEEM SORT OF CHILDISH BEING

THE YOUNG MAN YOU ARE NOW

BUT AS YOUR GOD MOTHER I HAVE A RIGHT TO BE A LITTLE MUSHY PAL!

I HOPE YOU LISTEN TO MY ADVICE; AND JEFFERY I'VE BEEN VERY PROUD

I'VE HAD THE HONOR OFBEING GOD-MOTHER

TO SO WONDERFUL A CHILD!

MAY I REMIND YOU SON WHAT THE HEAVENLY FATHER'S GIVEN YOU;

A WONDERFUL HOME. PROTECTION, LOVING AND GIVING PARENTS.

BE THANKFUL AS INTO YOUNG ADULTHOOD YOU ARE WHIRLED;

BETHOUGHTFUL OF THEM, REMEMBER, YOU ARE THEIR WORLD.

YOU ARE THEIR ONLY SON, IT SEEMS ONLY YESTERDAY YOU WERE A BABE;

WHEN LIFE WAS SO HARD AND SO MUCH OF IT THEY GAVE YOU!

YOU ARE GENEROUSLY BLESSED BY GOD; YOU ARE SUCH A GIFTED CHILD.

SO AS YOU ENTER ADULT LIFE, REALLY GET IN

THERE AND MAKE THEM PROUD!

AS THE YEARS PASS ON JEFFERY, GIVE MOM

A LITTLE HUG NOW AND AGAIN,

GIVE DAD A PAT ON THE BACK, A BIG SMILE, AND BE HIS BEST FRIEND.

THEY WERE NEVER AS FORTUNATE AS THEY

HAVE MADE YOUR LIFE FOR YOU!

ALWAYS LOVE AND HONOR THEM DEAR, AS THEY

HAVE LOVED AND HONORED YOU!

"Grannies Hymn"

GRANDMA BENTLEY WOKE UP DREAMING AND SINGING
THIS SONG; IN 1973. SHE ASKED ME TO WRITE IT!

"I'M GOING TO HEAV'N!"
(CHORUS)
EVERYBODY OUGHT TO WANT TO GO TO HEAV'N, HEAV'N!!
EVERYBODY OUGHT TO WANT TO GO SEE
OUR LORD AND SAVIOR! (REPEAT)
EVERYBODY OUGHT TO WANT TO GO TO HEAV'N. HEAV'N!

"WHAT GLORY IT IS JUST TO THINK ABOUT
GOING TO SEE OUR LOVED ONES."
'JUST THINK WHAT IT WILL BE WHERN WE SEE
OUR FRIENDS AND LOVED ONES!'
"I DREAM'T I SAW MY HUSBAND STANDING THERE
IN HIS OLD HAT AND GRAY-BROWN COAT.
MY DEAR LORD WAS WAITING NEIGH THERE TO
GIVE US ALL A BRAND NEW CLOAK!

CHORUS:
I'VE GROWN OLD AND TIRED, MY HAIR IS GRAY.
I'VE BEEN READY FOR SOME TIME TO GO.
BUT SOMEHOW I'VE JUST BEEN HANGIN' ON FOR
SOMETHING I'VE JUST GOTTA' KNOW!
BEFORE I LEAVE THIS OLD WORLD OF SORROW,
HARDSHIP, TOIL AND FEAR;
WILL YOU ANSWER ME ALL MY LITTLE CHILDREN;
WILL YOU MEET ME UP THERE?

CHORUS

WILL YOU PUT YOUR HAND IN JESUS' STRONG

HAND, WALK WITH HIM ALL THE WAY?

E'RE I REST ON MY SWEET SAVIORS' BOSOM, TELL

ME; WILL YOU MEET ME THERE SOMEDAY?

I'M ANXIOUS TO JOIN MY HUSBAND AND LOVED

ONES NOW; I MISS THEM ALL SO:

PLEASE ANSWER ME MY CHILDREN, ARE YOU READY SOMEDAY TO GO TO?

SHE SAID IN HER DREAMS SHE SANG WITH THE VOICE

OF AN ANGE! SHE ADDED; "I NEVER HAD A

GOOD SINGIN' VOICE, BUT IN MY DREAM I SANG

SO PRETTY HONEY, JUST LIKE A' ANGEL."

"SHE ASKED ME TO WRITE IT UP FOR HER BEDCAUSE I

WAS GOOD AT WRITING. I TOOK NOTES AND

WROTE IS AS CLOSE AS I COULD TO HER WORDS.

"I Am Fortunate"

I AM FORTUNATE, I HAVE FELT THE DESERT SAND

SIFT THROUGH FINGERS OF MY HAND.

I TASTED SALT IN THE COOL OCEANS SPRAY;

WATCHED WAVES LEAP, SPLASH AND PLAY.

I HAVE GAZED AT STARS ON CLEAR NIGHTS;

WATCHED THE SUN RISE UP BRIGHT!

A COUSIN AND I ONCESAT MANY HOURS SINGINGHYMNS

ON GRANNIES PORCH, A-SINGING.

BESIDE THE KENTUCKY RIVER SAT GRANNIES SHACK;

NEWSPAPERED WALLS, OUT-HOUSE IN BACK!

LIGHTS STARTE DOTTING THE RIVER HILLS THERE;

MIDST THE DARK, TINY WARM LIGHTS OF CHEER.

AS THAT OL' KENTUCKY MOON ROSE O'ER HILLS SO

DARK; WE FELT GODS' WONDER IN OUR HEARTS!

AND OH HOW FORTUNATE HAVE BEEN I. I'VE

HEARD MY FOUR BABIES FIRST CRIES!

I'VE BEEN PRIVILEDGED TO WATCH MY FOUR CHILDREN

GROW: GRAND-CHILDREN TO KNOW.

I LOVE THE MANY FLOWERS GOD SEEDS: HE SENDS

BEAUTY 'MIDST THE WILD WEEDS!

BIRDS THAT SING AND FLY, TREES THAT GIVE THEM

NEST, WITH ALL THESE I'M BLESSED!

I PLAYED IN WATERS OF THE RIO GRANDE: AT

LAKE TAHOE BASKED AND SWAM.

I HAVE SEEN NIAGARA FALLS, GRAND CANYON AND HOOVER DAM

AT A CREEK, GETTING BAIT WITH GRAND-PA, I

FOUND A SWEET, MINIATURE WATER FALL!

IN A GRASSY COVE WATER RAN FROM THE CREEK AND

O'ER A TINY HILL: IT MADE A WATER FALL!

I AM MOST FORTUNATE FOR ALL THAT GOD HAS

BESTOWN; WHEREWITH I'VE SEEN, I'VE KNOWN!

GREAT IS "HIS" LOVE IN MY HEART, FOR TRUTH,

RIGHT AND GOOD; TO HOLD, TO BELIEVE:

FOR I WOULD LET MY LIGHT EVER SHINE FOR JESUS

WHO DIED AND IN MY HEART IS ALIVE!

HE SAID "FEED MY "SHEEP:" TELL OTHER SOULS! IN

MY HEART HE'S THE GREATEST GIFT I KNOW!

TO: MOUNT OLIVET CHURCH:

A THING SO VERY SPECIAL FEW WOULD UNDERSTAND,

IS THE SAME LOVE FOR AND OF CHRIST;

SHARED BY SO MANY, HERE AT MY CHURCH HOME.

I AM SO HAPPY AND SOP PRIVILEDGED TO

HAVE FOUND A GOOD OLD-FASHIONED, TRUTH TEACHING;

GOSPEL- SPREADING; FAMILY IN CHRIST.

ALONG WITH THE SAVIOR, YOU EACH GIVE ME JOY.

SO PRECIOUS IS HIS LOVE: SO PRECIOUS ARE

EACH OF YOU IN MY HEART!

"J D Bryant"

HIS NAME IS J D BRYANT, NO MORE NO LESS,

NOTHING ABBREVIATED, NOR A THNG LEFT OUT!

HE LIVES HIS WAY, NOT TO SUIT ALL THE REST

AND EARNS RESPECT WHENEVER HE IS ABOUT!

WHEN YOU MEET HIM, WELL; YOU HAVE MET A REAL MAN!

HE'S A MAN OF GREAT PATIENCE, HE'S A MAN OF GOALS:

A QUIET, DEEP MAN, UNIQUE IN ANY CLAN;

FOR HIS WORDS AND HIS DEEDS COME FROM THE VERY SOUL!

SOME MEN ACT ONLY FROM THE MIND, SOME THE HEART,

BUT J ACTS ONLY AFTER SEARCHING DEEP WITHIN;

AND WHERE ANOTHER MAN MAY MISS THE MARK,

CAREFULLY, WITH PURPOSE, HE HITS AGAIN!

NO MORE THOUGHTFUL HUSBAND COULD THERE EVER BE.

OH HOW HE HAS LOVED AND UNDERSTOOD HER ALL THESE YEARS!

NO FATHER COULD LOVE BETTER THAN HE;

NO GREATER A FRIEND E'ER WISH AWAY YOUR TEARS!

HIS SENSE OF HUMOR IS SUCH; DEEP JOY HE GIVES.

HE IS WISE; HIS ADVICE IS SOUGHT IN MANY WAYS.

HIS PRESENCE; PRECIOUS: HIS WAYS, ONLY HIS!

OVER AND AGAIN YOU HEAR THE MAN'S PRAISE!

JD BRYANT, NUMBER ONE; NO MORE NO LESS;

MANY MEN MAY SEEM GREAT BUT NEVER REACH A GOAL:

J, IN HIS QUIET WAYPASSES LIFE'S TESTS!

FOR HE GIVES WITH 'ALL' HIS HEART, HIS MIND, HIS SOUL!

"Joyces' Garden Bouquet"

HER HEART IS AS A GARDEN WITH MANY PATHS'
WHERE ROSES AND PERFUMED LILLIES GROW.
TINY WHITE BLOOMS OF "THE BABYS' BREATH"
BORDER VARIETIES OF THE VELVETY ROSE.

HOW SHE LOVES A FLOWER NAMED 'LILY'.
SHE CHERISHES THE WHITE ELEGANT FLOWER.
"OH THE SCENT!" SAYS SHE: "SO HEAVENLY!"
"ONLY GOD COULD HAVE PUT IT THERE."

GOD GAVE US SWEET FLOWERS TO CHERISH;
JESUS WAS CALLED "THE LILY OF THE VALLEY."
THE BIBLE HOLDS THE GREATEST OF MYSTERIES:
MYSTIC ARE THE FORM OF ROSE PETALS WE SEE.

THE LORD GAVE ME TIME, AND WISDOM TO SEE
JOYCE Y. RATLIFF HAS A FLOWER PETAL HEART!
HER LIFE STANDS PROUD FOR GOOD AND PURITY:
AS DOES THE LILY THAT SHE LOVES EACH PART.

HER STRONG FAITH, HER CONSTANT PRAYERS:

CREATE A HEAVENLY INCENSE, EVER TO RISE,

WENDING HEAVEN-WARD, TO OUR JESUS THERE!"

'TIS A SWEET AROMA FROM HER GARDEN INSIDE!

SHE LOVES THE FLOWERS, EACH SINGLE ONE!

SHE SO CHERISES THEM IN SUCH A SPECIAL WAY!

NOW AND THEN I HAVE GIVEN HER SOME,

BUT NONE AS SWEET AS HER HEARTS BOUQUET!

"Lord My Babies are Sick"

LORD, I'M NOT SO GOOD ANYMORE AT SAYING PRAYERS TO YOU.

BUT SEEMS YOU'RE THE ONLY ONE NOW I HAVE TO TURN TOO.

MY HUSBAND DOES ALL HE CAN DO EACH AND EVERY DAY,

AND I DO ALL I KNOW HOW IN MTY IGNORANT WAY.

NOTHEING WE DO SEEMS TO DO ANY GOOD, NO, NOT ANYMORE.

THAT'S WHAT I COME HUMBLY PRAYIN. TO YOU FOR,

IT'S HARD FOR ME TO BEAR MY LITTLE BABIES CRY,

WHEN THEY ARE SICK ND SUFFERIN' AND DON'T KNOW WHY.

THEY'RE GOOD, AND SWEET AS THEY CAN BE!

THEY'RE ONLY INNOCENT CHILDREN YUOU SO GRACIOUSLY GAVE ME.

THEY'RE NOT DEATHLY SICK….I'M THANKFUL TOO,

BUT IT'S ONE THING AFTER ANOTHER AND I

FEEL LIKE THE WORLD'S FALLIN' THRU!

MY FIRST LITTLE ONE HAS BEEN SICK OFF AND ON,

DOESN'T SEEM SHE'S REALLY BEEN WELL FOR SO LONG.

IT HURTS MEWHEN SHE TELLS ME HER TUMMY HURTS,

AND OTHER TIMES HAS SUCH A COLD SHE CAN HAREDLY BREATHE.

NOW THE BABYS' COME UP WITH A COLD IN HER TINY LITTLE CHEST'

SHE SEEMS SO AWFUL TINY TO BE SO SICK, MY BABIES WILL YOU BLESS?

PLEASE MAKE THEM WELL AND HAPPY AGAIN.

TIS NOT THEIR FAULT, THE EVILS OF MAN!

AND IF THEY'RE SICK FOR ANYTHING I HAVE DONE,

LORD LETMEDO THE SUFFERIN' SOME!!

UT LORD LET ME HAVE STRENGTH ENOUGH

TO CARE FOR MY SWEET BABIES TOO.

THEY'VE NO ONE ELSE TO CARE FOR RHEM BUT ME AND YOU!

YOU WATCH YOUR CHILDREN CONSTANTLY

BUT I HAVE TO HELP THEM TOO,

,

WITHOUT SOME HELP FROM YOU! AMEN!

"Misty Dawn"

MISTY DAWN, SO TENDER, PRECIOUS AND DEAR'
WIPE AWAY FROM YOUR PRETTY CHEEK THAT TEAR!
OH SO BUSY, BUSY, YOU FLIT FROM HERE TO THERE,
AS IF YOU NEVER HAD A WORRY OR A CARE.
YET UNDERNEATH; THINGS YOU SELDOM EVER SPEAK
HURT YOUR TENDER HEART AND ANSWERS YOU SEEK.
YEAR BY YEAR, DAY BY DAY, HOUR BY HOUR
I'VE WATCHED YOU GROW LIKE A PRETTY FLOWER!
I'M SO PROUD OF YOU; BEAUTIFUL, LOVING AND RARE;
SO MUCH I'VE BRAGGED, I'M SO PROUD; A WOMAN FAIR!
SO LITTLE I SEE YOU, SO SELDOM WE REALLY TALK,
YET IT SEEMS LIKE YETERDAY YOU LEARNED TO WALK!
SO TINY AND CUTE WHEN YOU TOOK YOUR FIRST STEP;
AND I DON'T BELIEVE YOU'VE EVER STOPPED GOING YET!
ABOUT TO GRADUATE, MY; WHERE DID THE TIME ALL GO?
SO MUCH I WANTED TO SAY, TO DO, TO GIVE TO YOU.
YOU TRUSTED ME LITTLE MISTY AT YOU FIRST STEP,
SO TRUST ME MISTY JUST A LITTLE WHILE YET!
LET'S SIT DOWN AND DISCUSS THE GRADUATION FOR YOU,
SO I WILL KNOW THINGS WE NEED TO HAVE AND TO DO.
WE'LL WORK IT ALL OUT TOGETHER, WAIT AND SEE MY PET;
DON'T TRY TO WORK THINGS OUT YOURSELF MISTY, NOT JUST YET.
ABOUT TO GRADUATE, AND TIMES SO ROUGH,
BUT GOD HELPED US THROUGH OTHER TIMES TOUGH!
AND WE'LL WORK THINGS OUT; GOD, YOU AND I.
TRUST ME FOR THIS MISTY BEFORE OUT OF THE NEST YOU FLY.
YOUR PROM DRESS WILL BE THE PRETTIEST ONE OF ALL;
YOU'LL BE SO BEAUTIFUL DAUGHTER, "BELL OF THE BALL!"

"Mother, I Remember"

IT IS ALWAYS SUCH A GREAT PLEASURE TO RECALL

THE GOOD TIMES BACK WHEN I WAS VERY SMALL.

I FIND I STILL CAN REMEMBER ALL OF THE THINGS

THAT FOR A LITTLE GIRL, HAPPINESS BRINGS:

THE TINY NEW DOLL; WHY IT SOMEHOW MADE YOU FEEL

AS NEEDED AND PRECIOUS AS YOU; "FOR REAL."

ALL THE BIRTHDAYS, CHRISTMASSES; THE JOY, THE TEARS;

HAVE ALL PASSED TOO QUICKLY THROUGHOUT THE YEARS.

BEST OF ALL IS THE MEMORY OF YOUR SMILE;

THE HUGS, AND SITTING IN YOUR LAP AWHILE!

FOR THESE CHERISSHED MERMORIES I THANK GOD ABOVE;

THE GREATEST GIFT FROM MOTHER IS HER LOVE!

NO MATTER HOW GROWN-UP, HOW FAR WE'RE APART;

I'M STILL "YOUR LITTLE GIRL," DOWN IN MY HEART!

AND OFT' AS I GO THROUGH LIFES' DRAMA,

MY HEART CRIES OUT, "I STILL NEED YOU MAMMA!"

THEN FOR A MOMENT I'LL STOP AND JUST PRETEND

THAT I REAH UP ONCE MORE TO TAKE YOUR HAND!

LIKE LONG AGO, I'M YOUR LITTLE GIRL ONCE MORE;

AND WE STROLL DOWN THE LANE, JUST LIKE BEFORE,

WITH THE SUN SHINNNG BRIGHT AND LIFE ERY GAY;

SKIPPING NOW AND THEN, FULL OF LIFE AND PLAY!

MY GIRLS IN BED, ME HERE IN MY PAJAMAS!

YES, STILL YOUR LITTLE GIRL NEEDS YOU MAMMA!

"My Lords' S"Andals"

MY SOUL OFT LEADS ME TO GROW CLOSER TO MY LORD.

I THINK HOW HE DIED FOR ME, AND I'M DRAWN FORWARD.

ONCE I WAS MOVED SO; MY SOUL TOOK THAT STEP AHEAD: I

REACHED OUT FOR JESUS, WHO FOR ME DIED AND BLED!

A SNOWY ROBE OF WHITE WAFTED AROUND HIM THERE. WITH

OPEN ARMS AND KIND EYES, HE BECKONED ME NEAR!

I FELT HE HAD LONG WAITED FOR MY SOUL TO YEARN: SO

THE GREATNESS OF HIS HOLY LOVE; I COULD LEARN!

MY EYES DROPPPED HUMBLY; IN HIS HOLY PRESENSE, GRAND! MY

HAND REACHED TOWARD THE SANDALS OF THE GOD/MAN!

OH WHAT LONGING OF HEART, HIS PRECIOUS SANDLES DREW.

THEN, WITH SILENT NOD, HE BADE ME WEAR HIS WORN SHOES!

I WAS FRIGHTENED, WANDERING IF I HAD WANTED TOO MUCH:

SHOULD I: A SINNER; THE PERFECT ONE'S SANDALS TOUCH?

HE KNEW MY THOUGHTS! AGAIN, BADE ME PUT HIS SHOES

ON. I WAS ELATED! HE'D HAVE ME, HIS SANDALS DON!

HE SOFTLY SMILED, WITH LOVE AND SADDNESS IN HIS EYES.

MY HEART WARMED; SO GREAT A POWER; TO BE SO KIND!

I STOOD IN AWE THAT JESUS WAITS ONE PACE AHEAD; FOR

US TO STEP FORWARD; AND TO US, SUCH GIFTS GIVE!

JESUS' SANDALS SLIPPED SO LIGHTLY ON, AND I WALKED THE

PATH HE AND THE APOSTLES TROD, AND TALKED!

I REACHED THE GARDEN OF SWEET PRAYER AND OF PAIN, A

DARK DANKNESS OF SORROW FELL; LIKE HEAVY RAIN!

"DEEP" WAS THE PAIN HE SUFFERRED TO LEAVE

THEM BEHIND. ALONE ON HJIS KNEES,

"MY LORD'S SANDALLS" CONT.

KNOWING HE WAS SOON TO DIE!

IT HURT THAT THEY SLEPT? IT HURT THAT THE ONE BETRAYED!

SORROWS AMASSEDD HEAVILY; AS MEEKLY HE PRAYED!

WHAT POWER, WHAT GREATNESS: BEYOND THAT OF MERE MANS!

HIS PATIENCE, HIS ENDURANCE; WAS PERFECTION GRAND!

I FELT INEPT; SO WEAK. HE BADE ME COME ALONG.

I GAZED AT HIS SANDALS IN AWE, THEN FOLLOWED ON.

THEN ENGULFED WITH COMPASSION; MORE THAN CAN BE

TOLD: FEELING LOVE, PITY; TOO GREAT EVER TO UNFOLD:

EMOTIONSS SO STRONG, I FALTERED BENEATH THE WEIGHT! NEXT,

FELT BURDEN NEAR CRUSHING; FOR MANS PAIN AND HATE!

THEN I FELT HIS PLEADING: HUMBLE, PATIENT AND KIND; THE

NAME "LAMB OF GOD," TOOK REAL MEANING IIN MY MIND!

HIS DEPTHS OF PAIN AND SUFFERING O'ER CAME ME SO; I

WEPT: HEARING HIS CALL OFTEN ANSWERED WITH "NO!"

LO! HE HAD NO MALICE, JUST PURE UNDYING LOVE! HE

SURELY WAS THE BLESSED SON OF GOD ABOVE!

GRIEF HE BORE SILENTLY! FOR US: HE CHOSE TO DIE! I

COULD TROD IN PAIN NO LONGER! HELP ME I CRIED!

HIS SANDALS WERE GONE! UNBURDENED, I LOOKED ABOUT!

HE LET ME STEP BACK; YET WAITS, I HAVE NO DOUBT!

HE DWELLS THERE, WITHIN REACH: TO EACH OF US A FRIEND. EVER

BIDDING COME, NEVER SURPASSING OUR STRENGTH, AS THEN!

TO GIVE OUR LOVE IN RETURN IS ALL THAT HE SEEKS: SO

HE CAN GIVE ALL TO US, EVER OUR SOULS KEEP!

"Thank You Pastor Dewayne Walker"

AH, HOW YOU DO GET EXCITED PASTOR WALKER

WHEN BRYAN STATION HIGH HAS A BALL GAME!

YOU COULD HAVE 'GONE FOR GLORY' AND IN THE WORLDS EYES

WON! YOU SOUGHT GLORY IN HEAVENLY SKIES!

"THANK YOU!"

YOU WED SANDY WEBER; NINTEEN SEVENTY NINE!

SHE'S STRONG YET FEMININE, PERFECTLY FINE:

PRETTY, AND PERFECT AND WILL STAY FOR LIFE!

IT TAKES A SPECIAL GAL FOR A GOOD PASTORS WIFE!

"THANK YOU"

YOU OBEYED THAT CALL TO BUILD THAT BIBLE CHURCH!

AND TOOK SANDY TO INDIANA; COLLEGE WAS FIRST.

AFTER THE BIRTHS OF BOTH YOUR FIRST AND SECOND CHILD:

YOU GRADUATED IN NINETEEN EIGHTY-NINE: "PROUD!"

"THANK YOU"

IN NINETEEN-NINEETY YOU WERE ORDAINED TO PREACH

THE GOAL OF A CHURCH ABOUT TO REACH!

YOU CAME BACK HERE AND DROVE A BIG OL' TRUCK TO FEED

THE FAMILY AND BUILD A CHURCH: YOU WOULD SUCCEED!

"THANK YOU"

THE LORD HAD PROGRAMMED YOU TO SUCCEED!

OUR ALL STAR MADE HIS MARK; READY TO LEAD!

ALREADY PRACTICED IN A CHILDRENS BUS MINISTRY;

AND KNOCKING ON DOORS, YOU WERE WHAT WE NEED.

"THANK YOU"

A THIRD CHILD HAD SLIPPED INTO THE FAMILY TOO

WHEN YIOU STARTED YOUR FIRST CHURCH ON WALLER AVE.

YOU WORKED HARD TO GET BUSSES TO BRING IN CHILDREN

TO HELP THE ONES WHO MOST NEED A FRIEND!

"THANK YOU"

YOU BOLDLY BUT SINCERELY ASK ONES YOU MEET;

IF YOU DIED TONIGHT DO YOU KNOW YOU WOULD GO TO HEAVEN!

THOSE IMPORTANT WORDS, ARE SO VERY PRECIOUS TO ME!

YOU SCORE AGAIN! SINCERITY AND LOVE THEY SEE!

"THANK YOU"

YOUR CHURCH HAS TO BUILD ON FOR ENOUGH ROOM FOR US ALL!

I PRAISE THE LORD FOR YOU; THE CHURCH; AND ITS' CALL:

THERE IS LOVE AND UNITY IN MT. OLIVET CHURCH!

MAY I SAY MT. OLIVET "ALL STAR" CHURCH!

SINCERELY: CONNIE COLEMAN

"These Talents I Give"

LORD.

THESE BE THE TALENTS I GIVE TO THEE

UPON THIS ALTAR WITHIN THY HOUSE:

TO USE TO WORK THY GREAT HARVEST LORD

IN SPREADING YOUR TRUTH YOUR WORD

OF TRHE ONES I KNOW, THEY BE THESE:

GIVING OF WHAT HUMBLE GOODS ARE SENT TO ME

TO USE IN WYS TO SPREEAD THE WORD.

USING TALENTS OTHERS HAVE GIVEN

TO ADD TO THE NUMBERS IN HEAVEN!

MY LIFETIME OF WRITING, THE TALENT YOU GAVE

I GIVE BACK TO YOU FOR USE IN YOUR WAY.

THE TALENT YOU GAVE OF ORGANIZING AND PREPARING

I GIVE FOR USE TO PAVE THE WAY WITHOUT ERRING!

MY PURSE, BUDGET IT TO FIT THY WILL.

THY TRUTH IN MY HEART, LET SPILL,

YES, SO THAST THEY WILL SEE IT IS REAL!

CHAPTER AND VERSE OF TRUTH AND WISDOM IN THY HOLY BOOK;

AS YOU'VE OPENED IT TO ME; DEAR FATHER LET IT GUIDE OTHERS!

THESE GIFTS AND OTHERS I MAY KNOW,

LORD HOLD THEM EVER TOTHEE, NE'ER TO LET GO!

THESE I FREELY GIVE; THIS FIRST DAY OF THE YEAR 1997,

TO USE 'TILL JESUS COMES TO TAKE US TO HEAVEN!

YOUR CHILD AND SERVANT: CONNIE COLEMAN

AND LORD, PROTECT ME FROM ALL EVIL! AMEN!

"To Thy Crystal Waters, Lead On"

I'M ANXIOUS TO TRAVEL, LEAD ON!
THOUGH THE JOURNEY BE ROUGH, I'LL GO.
PLEASE LEAD ME NOW LORD, LEAD ME ON:
TO WHERE THY CRYSTAL WATERS FLOW!

WHEN I GET THERE I'LL BE WEARY:
I SHALL COOL MY DUST TRODDEN FEET;
RINSE AWAY CARES OF THE JOURNEY,
THEN, OTHER TRAVELERS I'LL MEET!

THE PATH MAY GET DUSTY AND DRY
BENEATH THE HOT SCHORCHING SUN.
WEE'LL REACH COOL WATER, BYE AND BYE;
TO SOAK CONTENTED, VICT-RY, WON!

I KNOW LORD, THE WAY'S HARD, AND STEEP
BUT I'LL FOLLOW, THROUGH THE LAST MILE:
TRY NOT TARRY LONG THE WEAY; KEEP
ON THY PATH, DO MY BEST, AND SMILE!

PERHAPS I'LL MEET ALONG THE WAY;
FRIENDS TO FOLLOW 'LONG, ON THY PATH.
WE CAN RINSE OFF THE DUST AND CLAY
IN JORDANS' COOL, SWEET CRYSTAL BAATH!

HELP ME NOW LORD, AS I MEET FRIENDS,

TELL HOW YOU WASH THEM WHITE AS SNOW,

SHOW THEM THY PATH, HOW TO BEGIN;

AND BRING OTHERS, WHO WISH TO GO!

REACHING JORDAN, SO SWEET, SO DEAR:

ONE BY ONE, FEET AS HEAVY AS LEAD:

HE'LL WASH OUR PAIN, OUR HEARTACHES, CLEAR

VICT-RY WON, WORK DONE, NEVER DEAD!

"When The Circle Closes"

THERE IS A BATTLE RAGING IN MANY HEARTS
TODAY! ARE THEY AWARE OF WHAT THE
BIBLE HAS TO STAY?
"ONE" NAMED "JESUS" WHO IS GODS'ONLY SON: WAS CRUCIFIED;
DIED, THEN HE AROSE, DEATH'S VICTORY WON!
RISEN; HE GAVE A DUTY TO ALL CHRISTIANS: SOULS TO WIN!
HE STAYED HERE AWHILE, THEN ROSE TO HEAVEN AGAIN:
PROMISING "THE HOLY SPIRIT," WOULD BE WITH US TO STAY;
UNTIL HE RETURNED AND GATHERED US BACK ONE DAY!
"HIS SECRET COMING WILL BE QUICK AS A THIEF IN THE
NIGHT. IN WONDERFUL GLORY HE WILL APPEAR IN SIGHT!
GABRIEL WILL BLOW HIS GREAT TRUMPET TO LET US KNOW!
"JESUS IS COMING!" "THE KING IS COMING!" "IT'S TIME TO GO!"
GLORIOUS SIGHT WE'LL SEE; JESUS COMING IN THE SKY! A
PRIVILEDGE TO RETURN WIOTH HIM, AT HIS SIDE!
QUICKLY, OUR FINAL MOMENT ON EARTH WILL BE O'ER! WE'LLL
GO WITH JESUS; LEAVING NON-BELIEVERS AT THEIR DOOR!
IN THAT LAST MOMENT AS WE RISE WITH THE SAVIOUR TO
GO: IN AWE AT THE BLESSEDNESS OF HIS HOLY GLOW;
WILL WE BE PROUD OF THE LIFES' BATTLE WE HAVE FOUGHT? OR
WILL WE CRY FOR A LOVED ONE, TO WHOM WE DIDN'T TALK?
WHILE RISING UP WE MAY SEE A LOST, BEWILDERED OLD FRIEND;
WE NEVER TOOK TIMRTO TELL: LEFT THERE, LOST IN SIN?
WILL WE TAKE ALONG WITH US A REGRETFUL PAIN? BY WAITING
TOO SHYLY TO MENTION OUR SWEET JESUS" NAME?

UNBELIEVER; FACE THE BAATTLE BETWEEN EVIL AND GOOD!

LISTEN TO THOSE TELLING OF HIIS COMING; YOU SHOULD!

FOR WHEN THE CIRCLE CLOSES, YOU COULD BE INSIDE! WHEN

WE RISE TO HEAVEN YOU COULD BE THERE AT HIS SIDE

LEARN OF JESUS BECAUSE YOU HAVE A DEATHLY DECISION TO

MAKE! JESUS COULD RETURN TODY, DO NOT WAIT TOO LATE!

WHEN JESUS WAS CRUCIFIED, THEN SLOWLY HE DIED; YOU

WERE ONE OF THE MANY SINNERS HEAVY ON HIS MIND!

"OH PRECIOUS SAVIOR; I OFT' CRAVE HEARING GABRIELS' HORN;

OFT' PICTURE "YOUR GLORIOUS COMING;" YET FEEL TORN!"

"YOU HAVE BEEN SO GIVING, WINNING THOSE DEAR ONES' SOULS,

EXPANDING THE CIRCLE IN HEAVEN WHERE I WANT TO GO!"

"YET, THE FAMILY IS GROWING, THERE ARE STILL SOME LEFT

OUT: LITTLE CHILDREN AND LOST PEOPLE ARE ALL ABOUT!

"SOON LORD IT WILL BE TIME TO COME FOR ALL YOUR OWN: PLEASE

LET US FILL UP MORE OF THE CIRCLE BEFORE ITS' CLOSE!"

IS THERE A BATTLE RAGING MY FRIEND, IN YOUR HEART TODAY?

DO YOU HAVE JESUS WITHIN YOUR HEART; THERE TO STAY?

DO YOU KNOW HIS COMFORT, HIS LOVE AND CONSTANT CARE?

WHEN THE CIRCLE CLOSES WILL YOU BE INSIDE WITH US THERE!

Printed in the United States
By Bookmasters